TEXTILES:
A WORLD TOUR

DISCOVERING TRADITIONAL
FABRICS AND PATTERNS

Catherine Legrand

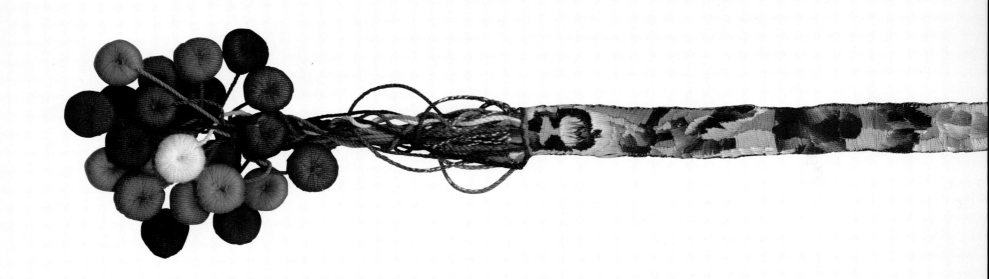

Contents

Introduction

'… such stuff as dreams are made on'

William Shakespeare, *The Tempest*

The first thing you notice when you travel is the way things look – a beautiful woman, for instance, passing in the marketplace, or a smartly dressed man working in a field. We can derive a great deal of pleasure from observing other people, noticing not only how similar they are to us, but also the ways in which they differ, admiring them and setting aside our prejudices in an attempt to understand them.

Our first reaction may be one of surprise. We come to realize that, despite the proverb, we do sometimes judge a book by its cover. The way we dress is an expression of who and what we are, whether that means Fulani or Yoruba, Hmong or Yao, Tzotzil or Quechua,

wife or widow, farmer or shopkeeper, nun or refugee, Hindu or Muslim.

Clothes fulfil many functions. They protect and conceal our bodies; they contribute to our comfort and express our sense of beauty; but they also serve as a badge of social identity. Colour, shape, fabric and decorative details all provide codified information. A particular headdress indicates a woman's social situation; a bag can tell us something about her ethnic origins; the colour of a tunic corresponds to an individual village; jewelry is an indicator of levels of wealth. Every detail is significant.

Garments too have their own lives and histories, and are the products of a range of

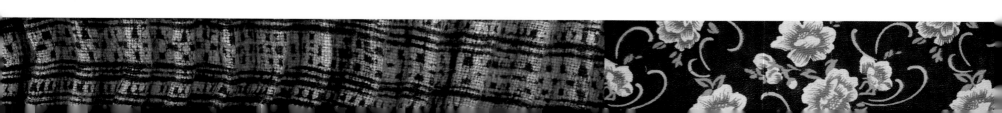

'Dress is a concept of the self that one wears upon one's self.'

Henri Michaux,
A Barbarian in Asia

processes. Plants are grown for their fibres, sheep and silkworms bred for their wool and silk, and the raw materials thus obtained are spun, woven, crocheted, dyed, felted, pleated, embroidered, lacquered, printed and sewn in a whole range of imaginative ways.

This book is a journey through several countries, all selected for their strong textile traditions and their styles of dress. Travelling through its pages, from one continent to the next, you will learn about how individual garments are made, observe similarities in cut and technique and be staggered by the skill and creative invention that can go into dyeing, weaving and decorating.

This book bears witness, in a modest way, to a world of infinite riches – a world which still survives, albeit at the risk of yielding to the lure of all things modern, or of becoming little more than a quaint archaism that survives for the benefit of tourists.

I wanted to stitch this book together like a beautiful garment, from a patchwork of sketches, photographs and stories. I hope it succeeds in passing on the sense of wonder that prompted me to embark upon this world tour in the first place.

CHINA

Meovac
PUPEO, NUNG, LOLO
YAO, HMONG

HA GIANG

RED YAO, XA PHO
NUNG, PHULA,
FLOWERED HMONG

LAKE BA BO

Muong
Te

HANI, BLACK YAO,
BLACK HMONG

LAO CAI

RED RIVER

LO RIVER

Bin Ho

LAI CHAU

LU, LAO, YAO LANTEN

VIETNAM

Phongsaly

NAM OU

HMONG, BLACK
TAI, HANI, LAHU,
WHITE HMONG

SON LA

Muang Sing

HANOI

BLACK TAI, LANTEN, AKHA,
TAI NEVA, HMONG

DIEN BIEN PHU

BLACK RIVER

BURMA
(MYANMAR)

RIVER KOK

Luang Namtha

HOA BINH

LAHU SHI

KAREN, LISU,
AKHA

MEKONG

Luang Prabang

CHIANG RAI

LAOS

GULF OF
TONKIN

CHIANG MAI

NAM NGUM
RESERVOIR

VIENTIANE

MEKONG

THAILAND

KWAI

Vietnam, Laos and Thailand
Many peoples, many styles

North Vietnam and the northern pasts of Laos and Thailand form a mountainous region on the borders of China and Burma that shelters a whole mosaic of different ethnic groups. These minority mountain peoples, or hill tribes as they are known, came originally from China and live alongside the national majorities, the Kinh, Lao and Thai people.

During the course of their migrations, these minority peoples have preserved their languages, customs, beliefs and traditional styles of dress. They are identified by these styles of dress, each group being distinguished from the rest by its costume, jewelry and headdress, and by a name associated with a colour or other clothing characteristic: Red Yao, Flowered Hmong, Black Hmong, White Hmong, Black Tai, White Trouser Yao, and more.

This chapter wanders through these different communities, from the villages of the Black Hmong women of North Vietnam to those of the Lanten, the dyer-women with their blue-stained hands, in Laos. It takes us past the paddy fields where the Hani and the Lahu are busy weeding, instantly recognizable in their multicoloured sleeves, and to the market places of Vietnam, where we encounter the red pompom-festooned headdresses of the Red Yao, the indigo turbans of the Black Yao, the long-line jackets of the Lu and Lao women, and the many-pleated skirts of the Flowered Hmong.

The clothes are made by the women. It is the women who harvest and weave the hemp, breed the silkworms, apply the indigo dye, produce the batik designs, embroider and sew the garments and decorate them with pompoms, shells and sequins.

For generations, the same techniques have been passed down from mother to daughter and used to make trousers, skirts, tunics, aprons, leggings, headdresses and bags, and headgear and clothing for children. The skill and imaginative flair that goes into this work makes each and every item unique. The embroideries depict tribal legends; the length of a pair of trousers indicates the wearer's village of origin; the colour of a pompom denotes the hill tribe to which she belongs; a headdress reflects her age or social standing. Their daily lives are harsh, but these women still manage to preserve a wealth of aesthetic traditions and techniques that have been handed down from their ancestors.

These women are my muses, the inspiration behind many of my own designs. I have created a cultural mix and match, reinventing the Flowered Hmong skirt, combining flowery Chinese cottons with indigo linen, assembling stripes and ribbons and braids to make sleeves in the style of Hani costumes. All that these designs are missing is the bright green backdrop of the paddy fields.

Painstaking pleats and breathtaking blues

The skirt of a thousand pleats
The Flowered Hmong and White Hmong of Vietnam

The very first time I went travelling, I came across some Hmong women, working in the fields beside the track that winds up from the station at Lai Chau to Sa Pa. In their bright skirts, they looked like flowers scattered across the hillside. I had never heard the name Hmong before, and knew nothing of their people, but it was in that moment that I suddenly had the idea of keeping a travel diary that focused on clothes and costumes.

Layers of beauty

The image opposite shows a traditional skirt bought in the market at Bac Ha, in Vietnam, designed to wrap around the waist and fastened with two ties. It is made up of three horizontal tiers of cloth. The first of these is in plain indigo linen. The second is a wide band of batik decorated with a criss-cross pattern of red braid and an appliqué of inverted squares. The third is embroidered in cross stitch and decorated with an appliqué of squares in plain and floral cotton.

The top strip has a hundred pleats, the second two hundred: each pleat in the first band has two corresponding pleats in the second, so that there is less fabric at the waist, but the skirt remains full. The Hmong women of the Meo Vac region buy imported skirts made of black synthetic material that is machine pleated; the White Hmong use raw fabric and pleat it themselves by hand, and the Akha women of Laos wear short indigo-coloured skirts. Over the border, in China, the skirts of the Miao women are made up entirely of batik or calendered to give them a purple sheen. In the Western world of high fashion, the pretty pleated wrapover skirts designed by Kenzo in the 1970s and 1980s became a fashion sensation.

It is said that it was the sight of an open latania leaf (left) which inspired a Flowered Hmong woman to make the first 'skirt of a thousand pleats' (opposite). The latania is a type of palm with large fan-shaped leaves. These are dried and woven together to make roofs and the conical hats worn in South-East Asia as a protection against sun and rain.

When an item of clothing wears out, it is taken to pieces and the worn sections are replaced while the bands of batik and embroidery are saved and reused. This also provides an opportunity to bring a garment up to date.

The Can Cau market is held on Saturday mornings, away from the villages, in the middle of a field. It provides an opportunity not just to buy fabric and clothes, but also to meet up with friends and the young Flowered Hmong girls dress up specially for the occasion. These gathered skirts are the equivalent of our ready-to-wear fashions.

Pleating secrets

The traditional hemp skirt may be known as the 'skirt of a thousand pleats', but the real number of pleats is two hundred or so.

'I did the pleating by hand and fitted the skirt round a straw hoop net. To stiffen it, I poured a mixture of water and rice starch over it,' explains the vendor. 'The skirt has to be left for a month. Then I sewed the top of the pleats and secured them with a tight chain stitch. One thing you absolutely must remember is to roll it up like a sausage and tie it together with the belt fastenings when you put it away.'

But fashions change and pleats are now being replaced by looser gathers: gathered skirts like the ones on sale in the markets at Bac Ha, Coc Ly and Can Cau are quicker to make and very popular with younger women.

Right: Coc Ly. Flowered Hmong women on their way home from the market.

Below: Young women from the White Hmong tribe in Sin Ho region. They go in groups to the market, which is the best place for both shopping and for meeting the opposite sex.

The White Hmong skirt: white and pleated

One of the most delightful sights is that of a young girl returning from the market with her skirts swinging as she walks. Whether she is Vietnamese, Laotian or Thai, it is clear that she is a member of the White Hmong tribe, a name that is owed to her natural-coloured pleated skirt. Nowadays, this is sometimes replaced by a pair of black trousers.

The skirt is made of cotton or ramie (*Boehmeria nivea*), a plant belonging to the same family as the nettle. It is harvested throughout the year and spun like hemp, but when woven produces a lighter and softer fabric.

Two aprons, one in front and one behind, protect the skirt. The White Hmong are experts in the technique of reverse appliqué, which they use to decorate their collars and their aprons.

Clothes of the Flowered Hmong, Vietnam

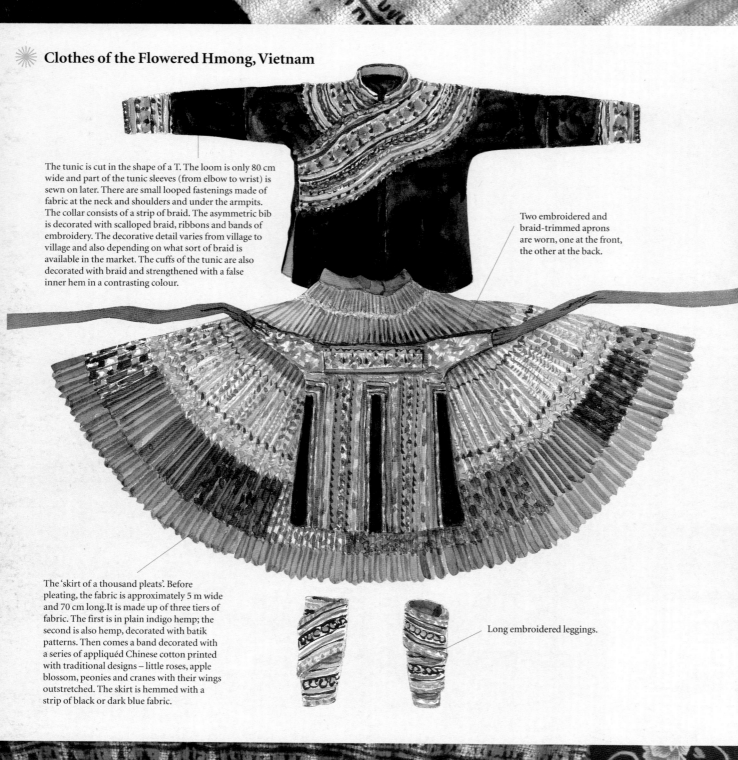

The tunic is cut in the shape of a T. The loom is only 80 cm wide and part of the tunic sleeves (from elbow to wrist) is sewn on later. There are small looped fastenings made of fabric at the neck and shoulders and under the armpits. The collar consists of a strip of braid. The asymmetric bib is decorated with scalloped braid, ribbons and bands of embroidery. The decorative detail varies from village to village and also depending on what sort of braid is available in the market. The cuffs of the tunic are also decorated with braid and strengthened with a false inner hem in a contrasting colour.

Two embroidered and braid-trimmed aprons are worn, one at the front, the other at the back.

The 'skirt of a thousand pleats'. Before pleating, the fabric is approximately 5 m wide and 70 cm long. It is made up of three tiers of fabric. The first is in plain indigo hemp; the second is also hemp, decorated with batik patterns. Then comes a band decorated with a series of appliquéd Chinese cotton printed with traditional designs – little roses, apple blossom, peonies and cranes with their wings outstretched. The skirt is hemmed with a strip of black or dark blue fabric.

Long embroidered leggings.

Above: Ky, a young Hmong girl in her colourful clothes. She has decorated her tunic with a brightly coloured fringe of plastic beads and sequins. She is also wearing a gathered skirt.

Below: Fanned out like skirts, sticks of freshly made incense are laid out to dry in the sun.

The Hmong tunic *Variations on a theme*

The countryside round Sa Pa disappears under a heavy tropical downpour. But taking shelter in this comfortable and welcoming home is like stepping into a game of 'Happy Families': here are grandmother and grandchildren, mother and daughter, daughter-in-law with her own daughter and baby son in her arms, plus a shy teenager.

One family: three women, three girls, and three styles of tunic. Despite their limited resources, all of them take great care of their appearance.

While keeping an eye on the younger children, the grandmother is also busy skinning hemp, a skein of which is wound around her waist. Her short tunic is trimmed with braid at the collar fastening and round the upper arms. She is also wearing an indigo skirt and smooth velvet leggings tied with ribbons, and a pair of huge hoop earrings. The t-shirt under her tunic contributes to the layered effect and looks fashionably modern. Her granddaughter carries the youngest child on her back and is wearing a pair of short trousers, a tunic and a braid-trimmed apron.

Far left: Little Kim is wearing a plastic headband and earrings, a pretty tunic, flowered belt, indigo apron and skirt with decorative appliqué. She looks exquisite.

Centre: The mother of the house is expecting another baby. She is wearing a short blouse like her own mother, while her little daughter is dressed in a tunic made from synthetic velvet patterned with flowers.

Left: The teenager is wearing a different version of the Hmong tunic, trimmed with braid at the wrists rather than the armholes.

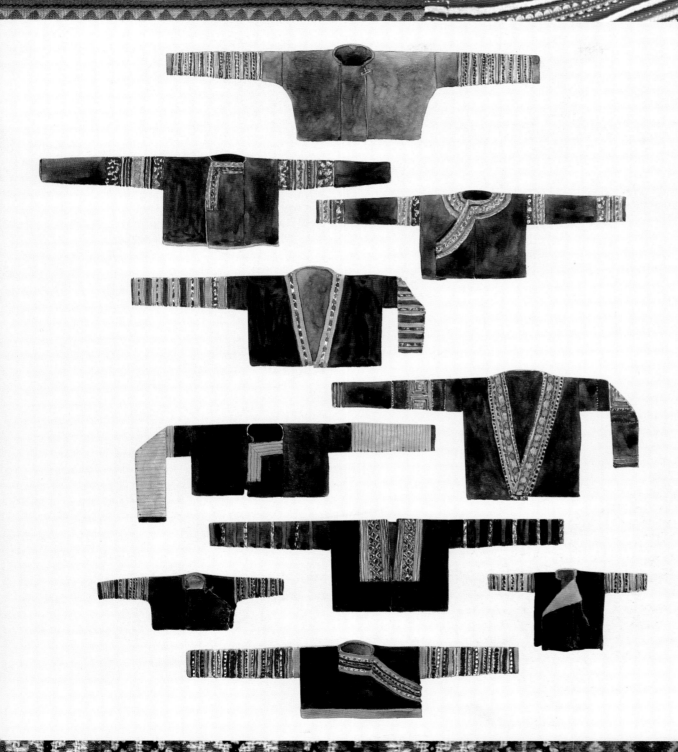

Above: A colourful velvet tunic hanging out to dry.

Below: The daughter-in-law, Hang Thi May, wears a striped jumper and, over the top, a V-neck tunic decorated with machine-made braid and fastened with a safety pin.

Indigo *The unifying blue*

Indigo comes from a magical family of plants that encircle the world like a green belt, passing via Africa from Guatemala to Japan. This bright green plant, once fermented, begets an infinite variety of blues. Across the frontiers of South-East Asia, indigo forges a link between different ethnic groups, creating an underlying unity of dress. The Lanten in Laos and the Black Hmong of North Vietnam, two minority groups, differing from one another in origins, language and costume but connected by the same blue, here provide an introduction to the life cycle of the indigo plant.

Right, top: Indigo, gang in Hmong. In South-East Asia, the two main varieties of indigo are *Strobilanthes flaccidifolius* and *Polygonum tinctorium*.

Right, centre: Lanten women wear their hair in a tight chignon, held in place by a silver pin. Around their heads, they wrap an indigo scarf with an edging of undyed thread.

Right, bottom: Aesthetics demand that the blue be very dark. The effect is lightened by contrasting jewelry, fastenings and belts and magenta-coloured pompoms.

Opposite: August is the month for indigo. Here, a Lanten woman returns to the village of Ban Nam Dee, carrying a heavy basketload of greenery on her back.

Harvesting indigo with the Lanten women of the Luang Namtha valley

The bitter smell of indigo hangs over Ban Nam Dee. The place is a hub of activity thanks to the constant to-ing and fro-ing of women leaving the village with baskets on their backs and returning, bent double under a heavy load of greenery. Following in their footsteps involves crossing a number of fords, weaving through plantations of sugar cane, struggling along the levees that border the rice fields, feet deep in mud, and climbing the hillside, up to the indigo plantations. The women are up there, blue silhouettes among the tall green stems, their pruning knives in their hands, cutting the plants that slash at their feet, filling their baskets. In the muggy monsoon season, the harvest is at its peak. Along by the river, where the baskets are unloaded, the atmosphere is buzzing. The leafy stems of the fresh indigo plants are bent in half and submerged in the vats, while the used plants that were steeping are thrown out on the bank. The women keep busy, helped by their children, who are only too happy to splash about in the blue water. They add powdered lime to the vats to accelerate the fermentation process by increasing the oxygen content. And then comes the dying, during which old faded garments, skeins of cotton and new lengths of raw cloth are immersed in the solution. The process is repeated twice more until the bright blue turns almost black and the village disappears under garlands of cloth, hanging from bamboo drying frames like the sails of a huge ship. Faithful to the etymology of their name – the Chinese for indigo is *landian* – the Lanten women are involved in an endless round of weaving and dyeing, producing clothes for the whole community and selling the surplus to other minority groups or exchanging it for other goods.

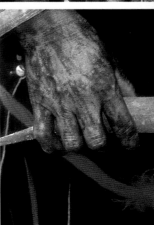

While she fills the vat, Li Su reveals some of the many facts and stories associated with the magical dyeing process.

'Little bits of paper soaked in the jar will bring good luck. Indigo has a persistent smell that stops snakes and poisonous insects from biting. When someone dies in a house, you have to wait until that person is buried before you start dyeing again. It's bad luck for a pregnant women to go near a barrel of indigo: she's likely to interfere with the fermentation. For the same reason, you mustn't say anything bad anywhere close to a vat.'

Dyeing instructions from Lo Su May

A young Red Yao woman from Sa Pa, from the accounts collected by Claire Burkert and Vo Mai Phuong:

'Soak the fresh leaves and stems of indigo in a large vat of water; stir occasionally to increase the oxygen content, and four days later take the leaves out. Tip three bowls of lime into the vat (one gram of lime to ten kilos of indigo leaves) and stir. Ash from rice straw or urine can be used instead of lime, which acts as a mordant or fixative.

Once the decoction has settled and the sediments have collected at the bottom of the vat, draw off the remaining water by filtering it through ash. Then mix the sediments with the ash. Add some more indigo leaves and water and leave to steep for seven to ten days.'

Harvesting, spinning and dyeing hemp with the Black Hmong women of Sa Pa

Sa Pa, the former French colonial residence of Haut Tonkin, lies in the shadow of Fan Si Pan (3,143 m), only 380 km from Hanoi and just across the mountains from the Chinese province of Yunnan.

These lands are the domain of the Black Hmong or Hmong Den, whose womenfolk look as if they have soaked themselves from head to foot in a vat of indigo dye. Their clothes are deep blue, set off by the glitter of silver jewelry. Their hands are blue from soaking cloth in the dye, and their calves are stained blue from their leggings. Their clothes give off the typical, slightly bitter smell of the dye, mixed with the smell of wood smoke from the household fires. Rain falls on the mountains and the paths are deep in the kind of mud that weighs like lead on the bottom of your shoes. Wrapped in a plastic sheet and armed with a small nylon umbrella and plastic sandals (or barefoot), the Black Hmong face the vagaries of the weather with stoicism.

The mountain peoples of these regions used to be very isolated, each community making its own

Above left: The glossy sheen of this young woman's waistcoat contrasts with the matte fabric of her coat and creates a subtle range of shades from ink-blue to violet. After dyeing, the cloth can be wetted with water to which plants and bark have been added, then beaten with a mallet to give it a shiny look: this process is known as calendering.

'I spread on some egg white and beat the indigo hemp on a wooden block to crush the fibres and give them that glossy look.'

textiles by cultivating hemp, cotton and ramie. Today, the Black Hmong are one of the few groups who continue to maintain their independence, planting and harvesting, weaving, dyeing and sewing hemp, while other minorities in the region now resort to buying or bartering their fabrics. Every Black Hmong house has its own little plot of land where hemp (*Cannabis sativa*) and indigo are grown, and every girl weaves her own wedding trousseau, learning the necessary skills from her own mother.

The yarn is bleached with lime and boiled in wax, then stretched on to a huge reel and woven on a horizontal wooden loom equipped with four pedal-operated heddles.

The weaving is done in the autumn and winter months when there is less work to do in the fields. The cloth is 4 to 5 metres long and rarely more than 40 centimetres wide. The narrow bands are sewn together to make garments specially adapted to this narrow cloth width. Very few women own a sewing machine, so the work is basically done by hand. Once the weaving season is over, the loom can be dismantled and stored between two roof beams.

In Van Thi Rê's house, Ta Phin, North Vietnam

Van Thi Rê lives in a village in the valley of Ta Phin, which the Black Hmong share with the Red Yao and the Tai tribes. Like her neighbours, she has her own indigo vat, which she uses on a daily basis to dye clothes. The result is an infinite range of shades of blue, produced by repeated washing, wear and tear and the different qualities of the woven cloth.

Life here in this valley is strikingly frugal. People have no furniture or knick-knacks, just a household altar where they honour their ancestors, a plastic mirror, a rice bowl and – in the local shop-cum-café – a single television, like a telescope directed towards the outside world.

The plain cut of the clothes and the solid colours are reminiscent of modern Japanese designers: the Hmong women, it seems, can teach us a thing or two about stylish simplicity. Sitting with her friends on little stools around the fire, Van Thi Rê is embroidering a *long tra*, one of those ornate collars typical of Hmong coats and waistcoats.

At my request, she tells me the names of all the garments hanging to dry above the fire.

Tha Thu Di smiles cheekily at the camera, with a flash of her gold teeth (she has four in total). She is stripping a skein of hemp and winding it round her hand, and wearing over her shoulder a type of woven basket used by all the smaller hill tribes of North Vietnam. Tha Thu Di describes her method for growing hemp, or *mang* as it is known in Hmong.

'I sow the hemp in March after clearing the ground and burning the old stuff, and harvest it in August after it has flowered, when the plants are about two metres tall. I pull off the leaves and leave the stems to dry in the sun for a week. I keep turning them every couple of days to make sure they dry properly, then I separate them lengthwise with a blade or my fingernail to extract the fibres. The stems are then soaked in boiling water with ash added. After that, I beat them to soften them. I wrap the fibres in a skein round my waist, then gather them together end to end and wind them into a ball – which is something I can do at any time, particularly when I'm walking.'

This process, known as retting, destroys the pectin that holds the fibres together.

Above centre: At a bend in the path, on the edge of a hamlet, three children perch like birds on a couple of leaning bamboo canes. The eldest, perched at the highest point, is doing some sewing; the little boy is trying to shoot birds with a catapult.

Black Hmong clothes, Vietnam

A headdress, *phô*, made of a hoop woven from fine bamboo, covered with blue cloth and held in place by a comb or hairslides, around which a long strip of hemp is wrapped. The hair is held in a tight chignon.

A sleeveless gilet, *chaté*, the same length as the coat, lined with blue cotton; the collar is embroidered with cross stitch and sewn on later.

A hemp coat, *chacô*, with long sleeves, edged with red chain stitch and lined with blue cotton.

Two wrap-around leggings, *côchiû*, in hemp or short-knap velvet. They are held in place with laces and protect the calves from thorns and the cold. They tend to fall down and a woman bending down to adjust her leggings is a common sight.

A pair of short trousers, *tri*, sometimes not much more than shorts, in plain hemp.

A belt, *lang*, a narrow band of hemp with two patterned sections echoing the collar design.

Opposite, inset: In front of a wall built from mud and rice straw stands a ceramic jar containing indigo dye. A large piece of bamboo bark serves as a funnel and a bamboo cane is used as a stirrer to keep the contents oxygenated.

Opposite: Van Thi Rê wears a double set of earrings and a silver torque. She talks about the dyeing process and explains:

'When the weather is overcast, the cloth is only soaked and set out to dry once a day, but as soon as the sun comes out, things speed up. When the cloth is dry, I soak it, and then re-soak it three, four or five times a day. I dye strips of approximately 15 sai each time. A sai is the distance between your two outstretched arms.'

Batik *Bo Y and Hmong skirts, Vietnam*

According to legend, a young Chinese woman was inspired to produce the first batik print when a bee dropped a few spots of wax in a vat of dye and left a reserve pattern on the cloth she was dyeing.

Finding another blue and white Bo Y skirt like the one displayed in the museum of ethnography in Thai Nguyên proves to be no small feat! Skirts, aprons, tunics and turbans: all the traditional Bo Y garments seem to have vanished into thin air. Bo Y women now put their costumes away in a chest for safekeeping and only get them out for the New Year celebrations and for weddings and funerals.

Today, Dang Thi Lu'ong is drying peanuts on an patch of beaten earth in front of her house. Simply dressed in trousers and an indigo tunic, she agrees to put on the garments inherited from her mother and bring the past to life just for a few moments.

'*The houses used to be surrounded by fields of cotton, which our mothers used to spin and weave,' explains Dang Thi Lu'ong. 'Today, that's finished. Now there are fields of rice and peanuts, which I harvest and sell in the market.'*

Above: This Hmong woman from Mai Chau is salvaging strips of batik from an old skirt.

Batik is used to decorate cotton and hemp. In the case of the Bo Y skirt, the strips of indigo batik are sewn horizontally on to a panel of plain fabric. The pleated skirt of the Flowered Hmong has strips of batik alternating with cotton prints and ribbons, and the batik is often embroidered in cross stitch and decorated with braid and appliqué to create a multicoloured effect.

atik, known as *laran* in Chinese,
s a wax-resist method of dyeing
hat has been practised in China for
nore than two thousand years. The
echnique derives from wax-resist
rawing, formerly done by hand but
nore recently involving the use of
pad. It is widespread among the
eoples of South-East Asia, where
: is closely linked with the process
f indigo dyeing.

   Using a charcoal pencil, the batik
rtist draws the designs on a plain
rip of cloth, attached to a block
f wood. Then she goes over the
harcoal marks with hot wax –
eeswax, stearin or some form of
lant resin – using a bamboo pen,
nown as a *ladao* in Chinese, with
copper nib attached which she
ips into the melted wax. She has
whole range of pens, depending
n the particular effect she wants.

   The designs are composed of
huge variety of traditional motifs
hat have been built up over the
enerations: chevrons, zigzags,
byrinths, spirals, swastikas,
ght-pointed stars, gourd flowers,
uffalo horns and more.

   When the design is complete
nd the wax has dried, the cloth
soaked in a bath of cold indigo
prevent the wax from melting;
nis process is repeated several times
n order to produce a really intense
nade of blue. The dye bath is then
rought to the boil; the wax melts,
nd as it cools, it rises to the surface,
here it forms a thin layer; this is
emoved and melted down with
ew wax when the whole process
repeated. The dye impregnates
ne cloth only in the areas that were
ee of wax, so the design appears
reserve, white on blue.

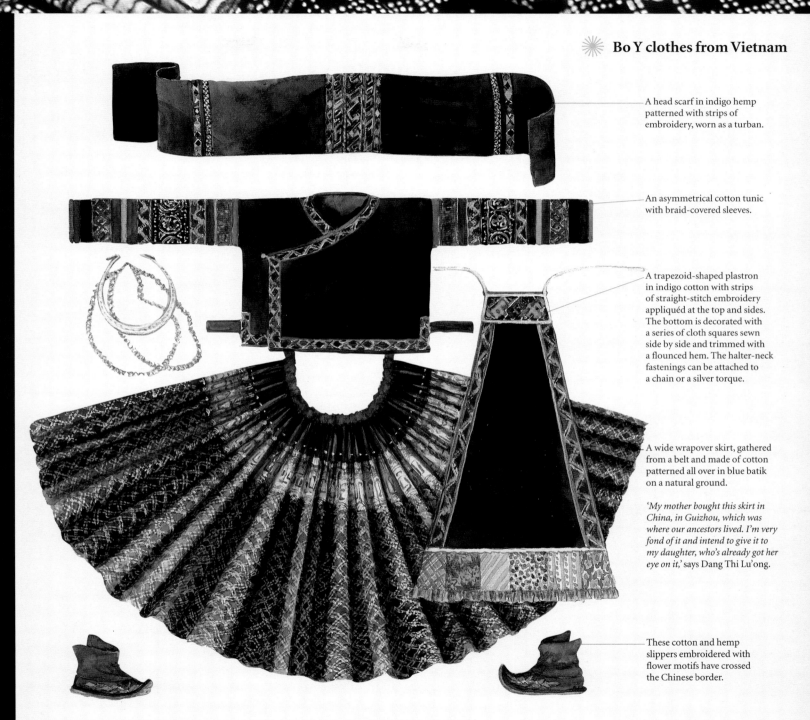

✳ Bo Y clothes from Vietnam

A head scarf in indigo hemp patterned with strips of embroidery, worn as a turban.

An asymmetrical cotton tunic with braid-covered sleeves.

A trapezoid-shaped plastron in indigo cotton with strips of straight-stitch embroidery appliquéd at the top and sides. The bottom is decorated with a series of cloth squares sewn side by side and trimmed with a flounced hem. The halter-neck fastenings can be attached to a chain or a silver torque.

A wide wrapover skirt, gathered from a belt and made of cotton patterned all over in blue batik on a natural ground.

'My mother bought this skirt in China, in Guizhou, which was where our ancestors lived. I'm very fond of it and intend to give it to my daughter, who's already got her eye on it,' says Dang Thi Lu'ong.

These cotton and hemp slippers embroidered with flower motifs have crossed the Chinese border.

 A language of stitches

Embroidery *The personal touch*

The Yao community is a little like a Russian doll: you think there's only one large one, then a second smaller one appears, and a third, one minority within another, and yet another. So it's not surprising that all the Yao women use something – an embroidery motif, a pompom or the colour of a turban – as a means of distinguishing their own group from the others.

The Yao family straddles a number of geographic frontiers: there are the Vietnamese Yao, the Laotian Yao and the Chinese Yao. And the Yao peoples have many names: the Red Yao or Yao Do; the Black Yao or Yao Den; the White Trouser Yao or Yao Quân Trang; the Tight Trouser Yao or Yao Quân Chet; the Yao Cham; the Yao Lantien Sha with their false braids; the Yao Tien with their silver coins; the Blue Dress Yao or Yao Tanh Y; and the Yao Ao Dai, with their long tunics.

Below: A Red Yao belt and scarf are hung to dry on a bamboo cane.

The root of a turmeric plant, which is used to produce a yellow dye.

May Me is a 16-year-old Yao girl. She lives with her family in a large wooden house built on piles on the side of a hill, surrounded by banana palms, bamboo and poinsettias.

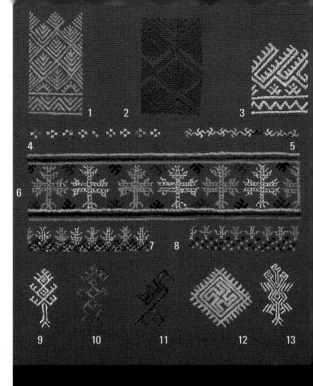

Red Yao embroidery

As you approach a Yao hamlet, you will see the women in their red headdresses sitting in the sun on bamboo stools, chatting while they keep their eyes on their sewing. The whole female population will be there, from tiny tots to grandmothers. The little ones, in their bonnets decorated with bells and pompoms, will be playing nearby.

Yao men learn to read and write their language (which uses Chinese characters), but the women are often illiterate. But their embroidery is a language of its own and they compose embroidered panels for their trousers and tunics as if they were wordless poems. Stitch by stitch, they embroider a unique creation and, alternating the red and yellow threads, they may depict a tiger's paw, a cabbage, a pine tree or the thunder, revealing the myths and beliefs of their people in pictorial form. They do their embroidery at any time of day, whether keeping an eye on the family buffalo or waiting for customers in the market, and they frequently work out in the open air to take advantage of the light.

Scarves and silks

May Me lives in a Red Yao village near Sa Pa. Her hair is caught up in a chignon and concealed beneath a red scarf. 'It's called a *ghong kau*. When I go to Sa Pa, I wear three or four *hong* – red scarves with tassels – on top of one another. I've been plucking my eyebrows and the hair on my forehead and temples since I was ten,' she adds when she catches me looking at the smooth expanse of skin on her forehead.

'I'm embroidering bands to go round the neck of my coat. I'm starting my wedding trousseau,' May Me explains, as she carries on with her sewing. 'My mother buys pure silk at the market in Lao Cai. It comes from China and it's expensive: 30,000 dongs [around $2] for a hundred grams. She washes it with rice water, to soften it, and uses water boiled with ash to fix the dye. When the thread is dry, we twist it first before we start embroidering.'

Yao embroidery motifs from the Ta Phin valley

Some motifs are derived from nature; others represent the Taoist balance between people and their environment. A woman belonging to one ethnic group may borrow a motif from another because it particularly appeals to her, and so the tradition evolves.

1 *tam xet xon:* used on trousers
2 *tam xong chiem chong*
3 a mixture of floral motifs
4 *diem muoi:* star
5 *pua cho sam:* little monkey paw
6 *choong:* fir tree
7 *xam nhan ton:* little plum
8 *tan xam nham:* peach blossom
9 *phan tho ton:* pine tree
10 *chen ton:* person
11 *no:* bird
12 *bua do chuan:* gibbon's paw
13 *dun chan deng:* banyan tree

Headscarves, or *hong*, are fringed rectangles of red cotton (70 x 30 cm) decorated with coins, beads, little bells and tassels. Yao women wear up to ten of these scarves draped in layers around their heads to create an impressively sized turban, each scarf symbolizing a level of wealth. The tassels are tied together to hold the whole thing in place. A young girl receives her first scarf when she starts courting.

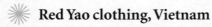

Red Yao clothing, Vietnam

The *luy dao* is a long coat made of indigo hemp, with slits at the sides. The two front panels are usually worn tied around the waist. From the waist down, the back of the coat, *luy khia*, is smothered with cross stitch embroidery, surrounded by a frame. Running down the middle of the back is a rectangular piece of embroidery, *luy tan*, which is partially obscured by the tassels, chains, beads, small coins and bells that hang from the collar.

The coat is fastened with a silver pin or a safety pin. The neckline is accentuated by a double band of embroidery, *luy leng*, decorated with tassels, *pay*, and beads, *cho*.

The belt, *sin ton*, is decorated with beads, tassels and little round bells. It is worn on the hips and tied at the back.

The plastron, *chap hong*, is a narrow strip of red cotton designed to cover the gap between the front panels of the coat. It ties around the neck and is decorated with rows of metallic beads and indented metal plates, and has an embroidered section at the bottom that hangs down from the waist like a narrow apron.

The trousers, *la peng*, are made of hemp and decorated at the bottom with several rows of embroidery. Short trousers are worn for working in the fields, long ones for market days and festivals.

Li Ta May is 77 years old and is May Me's grandmother. The panel she is embroidering in cross stitch will become the bottom of May Me's trousers.

'When I wash my embroidered trousers, the orange patterns fade to yellow, the indigo dye of the cloth runs into the yellow, turning it green, and the red becomes maroon: the colours are washed together, bringing the garment to life and making it beautiful' says Li Ta May, who, in common with the majority of Yao, has no problem with fading colours.

Right and below, bottom: The bride Ly Sai Nhan and her friends are busy finishing off her trousseau and wedding clothes. The pedal-operated sewing machine occupies pride of place in the little courtyard and the whole family is cheerfully occupied with cutting, sewing and embroidering.

Below, top: The bride's father is wearing the traditional Yao suit: a short jacket in indigo hemp, called a *chan lui* or *sua lui*, decorated with bands of embroidery at the wrists and on the back. A pair of plain hemp trousers and a long scarf, *goong peu*, wound round the head, complete the outfit, together with a felt beret, which he has chosen to wear instead of the traditional turban. In front of him is the new jacket he has just made for the wedding festivities.

At a bend in the path, we meet a group of Red Yao women carrying bags, backpacks, packages and presents, and dressed in their best clothes. 'We're going to Nam Tong, where there's going to be a wedding,' they tell us. The hamlet is buzzing and everywhere you look people are busy sewing.

In the wedding ceremony, every detail of clothing is significant, and the bride will be judged on both the skill and the beauty of her embroideries. The words of a popular Yao song say it all:

> 'She has been an excellent embroiderer
>   since she was a girl.
> She's a charming young woman,
>   worth her weight in gold.
> My family wants you to be our
>   daughter-in-law.
> I want you to become our dressmaker.'

Ly Sai Nhan, a member of the Black Yao people, wears her glasses tied to her turban with yarn. Many women develop eye strain and other sight problems that interfere with their embroidery. Some of them receive charity donations that allow them to get glasses.

Above: Meo Vac market, to the east of Ha Giang, is where the Black Yao gather on Sundays. These gatherings are very different from the colourful markets held by the Flowered Hmong: here the dominant colours are dark with just a smattering of green, electric blue and fuchsia pink. The dense, shifting crowd resembles patches of coloured ink escaping from spilt bottles.

Centre, top: A Yao woman works in the fields, exquisitely dressed – like a black tulip against the golden rice.

Centre, bottom: This Black Yao woman is on her way to the market at Meo Vac to sell incense. Her turban – a band of fabric wound round and round to create a huge flat disc – looks like an indigo halo. Her tunic is a symphony of blues, decorated with a triple row of embroidery.

The Black Yao women

Leaving Sa Pa to the west, we are no longer in Red Yao (Yao Do) country: we have entered the lands of the Black Yao (Yao Den), named after their indigo turbans. They are embroiderers of skill and commitment – a commitment demonstrated by Ly Sai Nhan (above), wearing her huge black turban and sitting perched on a rock while she works.

The town of Sin Ho is situated on a high plateau exposed to heavy rainfall. Sunday is market day, and despite the persistent rain, the place is transformed by an explosion of colours, costumes and smells.

The market serves as a focal point for communities scattered throughout the neighbouring mountains: the Hmong women with their impressive red woollen hairpieces, the dignified Yao Lantien, the White Hmong women in their pleated skirts and pointed hats, the astonishing Lu with their black teeth, the elegant Black Tai and Black Yao women in their voluminous turbans.

They all gather here: to sell sugar cane, Chinese cabbages, bamboo shoots, limes, ginger, papayas and bananas, to sell bee larvae, river crabs and dried fish, and to buy Chinese cottons, plastic sandals, indigo paste, metal ladles, rice wine, embroidery thread, beads and tiger balm. When the market ends, they rest on the benches of a stall selling soup (*pho*) – a bright array of turbans clustered together – before returning to their respective villages.

Black Yao clothing, Vietnam

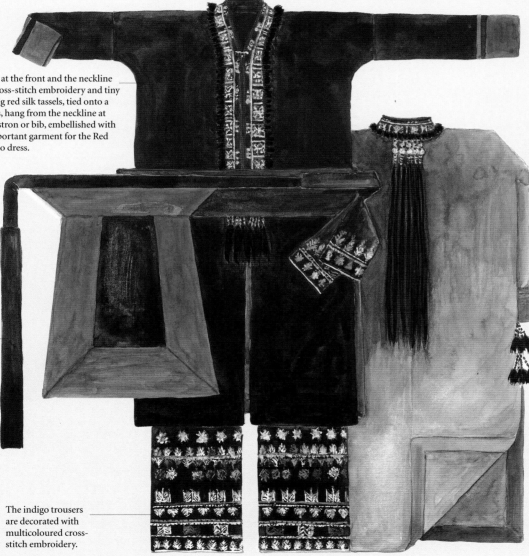

The turban is a band of indigo hemp about 8 metres in length wound around the head. The wearer's hair is held in a chignon and plucked to well above the natural hairline. Earrings, copper bracelets, a silver torque and a broad-strapped shoulder bag in blue cotton and flowered material complete the outfit.

The long indigo tunic is open at the front and the neckline is decorated with a band of cross-stitch embroidery and tiny red pompoms. Four to six long red silk tassels, tied onto a row of beads and metal pieces, hang from the neckline at the back of the tunic. The plastron or bib, embellished with small plates of silver, is an important garment for the Red Yao but is not part of Black Yao dress.

The apron is a rectangle of black hemp edged with broad bands of electric blue cotton. It is worn below the waist.

The indigo trousers are decorated with multicoloured cross-stitch embroidery.

Above, top: Market day at Sin Ho is over and these Black Yao women are preparing to leave with their laden baskets.

Above, bottom: This woman explains why Black Yao women pluck their foreheads: 'We keep up this tradition because hair is seen as a visual distraction: it prevents us from being able to admire the beauty of our clothes.' Throughout the centuries – from the Middle Ages to the reign of Queen Marie-Antoinette – large headdresses fpr women seem to have been regarded as beautiful, and the impressive turbans worn by these small mountain communities are a continuation of this custom.

White Trouser Yao clothing, Vietnam

The tunic, called a *way*, is made of indigo hemp and extends no lower than the knee. Neckline, shoulder seams, cuffs and mid-back seam are all delicately embroidered. The two front panels close edge to edge, held together by a braided belt, and there is a slit at each side going up to the waist, often accentuated with embroidery.

A woven braid serves as a belt.

The hemp trousers, *qua*, are short and plain. Indigo ones are worn for everyday purposes; white ones are reserved for ceremonial occasions. A small embroidered bag is worn at the waist, attached by a silver chain and containing a betel nut, betel leaves and a small quantity of lime, all of which the women chew.

The headscarf is a piece of indigo cotton, 45 cm square, hemmed with alternating red and white piping and decorated with a star motif, *fam tsing*, at its centre. A narrow woven fastening fixed at one corner is used to tie around the scarf and hold it in place.

A plain hemp plastron, *pan lang*, is embroidered with panels of green, black, red and maroon cross stitch with an eight-pointed star at the centre. The motifs are so varied as to suggest a great deal of imaginative licence within the accepted traditions. The plastron has no straps but attaches instead to the hooks of a silver torque. It is also backless, fastening at the lower back and always worn with a tunic over thetop. There is a small invisible pocket sewn inside the plastron.

A woman from the White Trouser Yao tribe

Their Vietnamese name is Yao Quân Trang, which means literally White Trouser Yao, and is not to be confused with the Yao Quân Chet or Tight Trouser Yao, a different sub-group. However, their white trousers are reserved for ceremonial occasions, and on a day-to-day basis, White Trouser Yao women are usually seen wearing indigo trousers!

But the most distinguishing feature of these tireless embroiderers is not the colour of their trousers, but their embroidered plastrons, sewn from raw hemp and decorated with tiny cross-stitch motifs, as well as their black-painted teeth. Silver necklaces serve as a halter necks for the plastrons, a couture touch that even Paco Rabanne would be proud of.

Right: This Yao woman has just been picnicking (on sticky rice flavoured with spices) by the field where she is planting mandarin trees. She is fitting in a bit of embroidery before getting back to work. The White Trouser Yao live in houses built on stilts, on well-irrigated land, surrounded by plantations of latania, betel and banana palms. They grow sugar cane, cassava, persimmons, citrus fruits and tobacco.

Seed embroidery

'Job's tears' are the long, slender, greyish-coloured seeds of a tropical grass, Coix lacryma-jobi. Harvested in autumn, they are either left in their natural state or heated until they turn white, and then they are threaded and sewn like beads. Since they occur naturally, they cost nothing, and are used by the Xa Pho in Vietnam, and by the Karen and Akha in Thailand, who intersperse them with cowrie shells.

Lon Chau, a Xa Pho embroiderer from Vietnam

It is drizzling in My Son, the Xa Pho hamlet, situated in the Nam Tong valley near Sa Pa. Lon Chau lives in a house of split and woven bamboo, and here, in the privacy of her home, she finally agrees to show us the embroidered blouse she keeps in a trunk, pulling it on over her pink t-shirt.

Noni, a Karen embroiderer from Thailand

The seeds that Noni is embroidering on to a striped blouse are known as 'Job's tears'. Her daughters, like most Karen women, harvest, spin and weave their own cotton, which they use to make skirts (*nî*), leggings (*cobô*), turbans (*copoki*) and blouses (*cheta*). The basic shape and rectangular cut of these garments is reminiscent of Mayan clothing but, like the Amerindians, Karen women compensate for the simplicity of both cut and fabric with elaborate decorative techniques. They use ikat threads to enhance the yarn of their skirts and embroider their tunics with seeds and mercerized threads, deliberately leaving the seams visible.

At the age of 86, Noni is still embroidering, even though it's sometimes a struggle to thread her needle.

 ## Xa Pho clothing, Vietnam

The turban, a long strip of indigo hemp, is replaced for everyday use by a plaid scarf.

The rectangular blouse of indigo hemp has a square neckline and is made up in two parts. The top section or yoke is embroidered with white seeds in star and stripe patterns. The lower band, around the abdomen, is entirely covered with geometric designs in red, orange and white in the shape of zigzags, steps and chevrons. A few delicate rows of embroidery are also used to accentuate the cuffs.

The long skirt is sewn from a rectangle of woven indigo hemp in the shape of a tube, rolled over at the waist and held in place by a belt. The skirt is traditionally embroidered with white, orange and red silk according to strict symbolic conventions: motifs include trees, triangles, steps and diamonds.

Above: Lon Chau

Amazing appliqué

The Lolo women from Vietnam are the uncontested queens of appliqué. Their traditional costumes are smothered in thousands of appliquéd triangles, assembled with the expert skill shared by all the seamstresses of South-East Asia, who enliven the simplicity of their indigo garments with brilliant decorative details. Whether the product of chance or instinct, culture or tradition, the colours are always harmonious, the proportions are perfect, and the workmanship is delicate.

The harlequin costumes of the Lolo

The village of Meo Vac, situated in a bowl surrounded by limestone peaks, is the scene of a Sunday market that is a melting pot for the region's ethnic groups, with Hmong, Black Yao, Nung and Giay women all exchanging their goods and parading a panoply of colours that must have been even more spectacular when the Lolo women still dressed in their flamboyant costumes. Now the thread of tradition has been broken and the Lolo women wear trousers and t-shirts that render them almost anonymous. However, with a little encouragement, Doâm Hông Mai and Dinh Hông Duyên, two villagers from Sang Pa'a, agreed to put on their costumes for us.

Small equilateral triangles (just a centimetre across) are appliquéd on to larger triangles to create a vibrant mosaic of brilliantly contrasting colours. The composition is reminiscent of Vasarely's op art paintings, and is unified by the repeated reds, the use of plain fabrics throughout and the choice of a triangular motif of unvarying size.

'The triangle represents the empire over which the Lolo people once ruled,' explains Thang Thi Sung, the grandmother. When asked how long it took her to sew the costume, she replies, evasively, '*xo miung*' – a long time.

❋ Lolo clothing, Vietnam

Opposite: Doâm Hông Mai and Dinh Hông Duyên:

'My mother gave me this costume when I got married. I don't wear it because I don't want to spoil it. I wouldn't know how to sew something like this: it's too complicated and would take too long,' says Mai.

A long indigo turban is worn wrapped around the head. The fabric is decorated with batik designs and appliquéd triangles and pompoms, embroidery and beads and edged with long fringes.

A short collarless bolero-style jacket in black and blue cotton. The front panels, back and sleeves are covered with brightly coloured appliquéd triangles – of which there are no fewer than a thousand! Plastic sequins are now sometimes added to a jacket to jazz it up – a sign of tradition adapting to changing times.

An apron, sewn from a large rectangle of black cotton satin with appliquéd triangles. It is hemmed with a row of multicoloured beads and is wrapped from behind the back, with the two flaps meeting in front of the trousers.

A pair of black cotton trousers decorated at the ankles with small appliquéd triangles and with patterns in reverse appliqué.

Two belts, one in blue, the other in white cotton.

Hani and Lahu tunics

This young Lahu woman is hemming a new tunic.

The long tunic, in black cotton, buttoned at the collar and under the arm, is slit at the sides and worn over a pair of straight trousers.

The tunic worn for everyday use has a plain front, whereas the ceremonial tunic is decorated with a sparkling arrangement of metallic beads alternating with silver coins: the quantity of coins indicates the social status of the wearer. The composition of beads and coins varies from village to village and recalls the decorative work of the Akha women from Laos.

Each sleeve of the tunic is made up of around forty strips of cotton. The effect is exuberant but controlled, the inclusion of black or white stripes introducing an element of discipline among all the flowered cottons, and alternating bands of blue and black providing a counterbalance to the multicoloured sections. Hmong and Yao women have incorporated this style of sleeve into their own way of dressing. Women are influenced by what they see one another wearing in the marketplace and styles evolve as a result. The cut and ornamentation of a garment are regulated by strict conventions, but there is still room for creativity – by modifying the pattern of sleeve stripes, for example, or by choosing how to position the coins on the jacket front.

The sleeve of this tunic is faded and falling apart. The effect is rather poignant and the wearer, a Hani woman, doesn't want to be photographed like this, and rushes back home to put on a new tunic.

Crayon-bright colours: the appliqué sleeves of the Hani and Lahu women

The long tunic worn by the Hani and Lahu women is not unlike the *ao dai*, the traditional silk tunic worn over trousers by Vietnamese women. The 'mountain' version is enchanting: made from indigo hemp, with multicoloured sleeves and a plastron glittering with beads and coins.

In North Vietnam, a track follows the right bank of the Sông Da, the Black River, from Lai Chau in the direction of China and Laos, traversing the territory of the elegant Hani and their neighbours the Lahu. The women no longer weave their own cloth today: the cotton they need to make their tunics, trousers and headdresses is now bought or obtained in exchange for other goods.

Right: Van Mi So, a young Lahu woman, wearing a brand-new tunic. The less well-off may own two or three different tunics; a wealthy woman might have around a dozen.

The Pupeo skirt with its multicoloured hem

Công Cha is one of the hamlets that are home to some of the seven hundred Pupeo, a small Vietnamese community. An old woman comes into view, walking round the side of a house. She is dressed in black cotton with a few contrasting splashes of colour. Her tunic is decorated with narrow strips of piping and her skirt is hemmed with a multicoloured band.

Above: For this photo, Giàng Thi Thien, wife of the village headman, has put on the beautiful silver necklaces that she inherited from her mother.

Opposite: An old Pupeo woman in front of a pink wall.

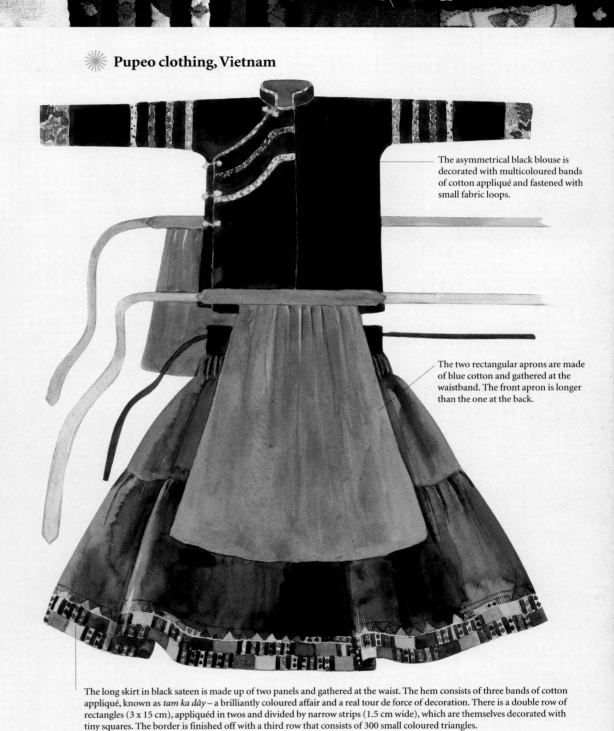

✳ **Pupeo clothing, Vietnam**

The asymmetrical black blouse is decorated with multicoloured bands of cotton appliqué and fastened with small fabric loops.

The two rectangular aprons are made of blue cotton and gathered at the waistband. The front apron is longer than the one at the back.

The long skirt in black sateen is made up of two panels and gathered at the waist. The hem consists of three bands of cotton appliqué, known as *tam ka dây* – a brilliantly coloured affair and a real tour de force of decoration. There is a double row of rectangles (3 x 15 cm), appliquéd in twos and divided by narrow strips (1.5 cm wide), which are themselves decorated with tiny squares. The border is finished off with a third row that consists of 300 small coloured triangles.

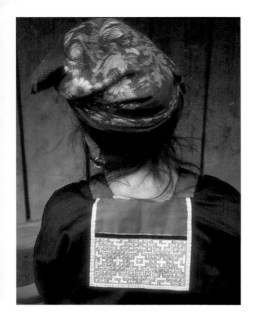

Hmong collars and belts: labyrinths of reverse appliqué

The sailor-style collars, apron flaps and baby slings worn by Laotian, Vietnamese and Thai women and by the White and Black Hmong are textile tours de force, like brilliant gem-studded mosaics. They are produced using a technique known as reverse appliqué, essentially the same technique that is used by the Kuna women of Panama to produce the blouses known as *molas* (see page 190). A layer of cotton is superimposed on another layer of a contrasting colour. Then a pattern is cut into the top layer and the edges are turned back under and sewn down to reveal the colour of the bottom layer as a reverse or negative pattern. Any number of designs can be produced using reverse appliqué – steps, spirals, labyrinths, chequerboards and more – with each motif outlined by tiny embroidery stitches.

Akha women: a bold look

Under a cloudy sky, Reinato, our Karen guide, uses a machete to open up a path for us and lead us to the Akha village situated on a ridge, its entrance marked by the traditional porch. With its predominance of thatch, bamboo and beaten earth, the village would be a relatively colourless place if not for the presence of the Akha women, whose coin-covered headdresses glitter in the sunlight.

These women wear very distinctive costumes: short pleated skirts and little aprons, open jackets and a bustier top, held in place by a single strap and exposing their navel and upper chest, together with a pair of leggings that accentuate their slim legs. The garments are all matching, made from rough indigo and black cotton, woven by hand and decorated with a scattering of embroidery, coloured cotton appliqué, beads, seeds, cowrie shells and coins. It is rare to see a complete outfit being worn at once: one woman may have left off her headdress; another will have replaced her jacket with a man's shirt, and another will be wearing a t-shirt instead of the traditional bustier. But for all this mixing and matching, an Akha woman can still be easily identified by the details she has chosen to retain.

Akeu, an Akha grandmother in her headdress and bustier, is carrying her grandson on her back. She tells us:

'I keep my headdress [mcheu] *on all week. I sleep in it. I use a silver pin that's stuck into the headdress if I have an itch, and I only undo the whole thing to wash my hair once every six or seven days.'*

She adds, mischievously:

'You see, the keys to my chest of valuables are attached to a ring at the end of the pin, so no one can steal them!'

✳ Akha clothing, Laos

The jacket, *pehong*, in indigo cotton. The armholes are decorated with bands of appliqué in a plain cotton that is either home dyed or bought. The blue, red and green tend to fade a little in the sun and harmonize well with the embroidery.

The wrapover skirt, *peedee*, in plain indigo cotton. The pleats are sewn into a belt.

The bustier, *lasha*, with a single strap that fastens at the front. The strap may be a simple piece of string or a more ornate affair decorated with a row of silver coins.

The leggings, *cubing*: two short tubes of indigo cotton covered with appliqué.

A belt, *dedong*, an embroidered bag, *peton*, matching the costume, a string bag, *kaya*, crocheted from forest vines and dyed indigo, an apron and a headdress, *mcheu*, complete the outfit.

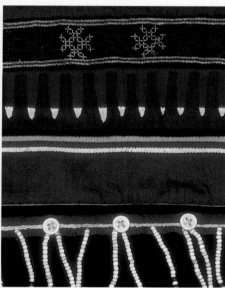

Above, top: This bride-to-be is going to Muang Sing with her fiancé and her sister. The two young women are wearing the traditional jacket and headdress and their silver jewelry, but a long Laotian-style skirt in place of the short hemp one. The man wears a traditional Akha suit – wide-legged indigo trousers and an embroidered jacket – but has swapped the turban for a cap.

Above, bottom: Loimi Akha women wear a small apron, a rectangle of indigo cloth (20 x 30 cm) with alternating bands of appliqué, embroidery, coins and seeds, a heavy fringe of seeds and glass beads, with pompoms and cowrie shells. The ethnologist Elaine Lewis suggests that the purpose of this apron is to cover the woman's thighs when she sits down, since the skirt itself is so short.

Wrapover jackets of the Lu and Lao women

The wrapover jacket or su'a is made of indigo hemp, fits closely at the waist, crosses over the chest and flares at the hips to form a basque. It is decorated with old coins, and appliqué and worn over a long skirt to create the effect of a tailored suit, giving these Vietnamese women a very contemporary look.

Tao Thi Seng (7) and Tao Thi On (8): two cheeky little princesses in traditional dress. Lengths of hemp can be seen drying in the background.

Opposite, above left: Vang Thi Sen has taken off her jacket in order to carry water up from the river. She is still wearing her turban and skirt, and the effect is both traditional and modern. She tells us:

'I've got a number of jackets: everyday ones that have been worn a lot and are trimmed with aluminium, and a good one for special occasions. It's like a dowry with sleeves. I'll happily sell you one, but I'll never part with my jacket with the silver coins!'

Clockwise from top centre: Silkworms feeding on mulberry leaves. Bamboo poles are still used, but plastic buckets have replaced wooden ones. The permanently blue hands of a dyer. Skeins of silk and an enamel bowl full of cocoons.

Opposite, below right: A mattress is drying in front of the house. Crouching on the terrace, two young girls are in the process of making a small indigo futon. They have quilted the hemp using large stitches and are stuffing the inside with soft white grass, packing it down with a bamboo cane. An overlapping band of striped fabric forms the sides of the mattress.

Opposite, below left: An embroidered jacket hanging out to dry on a bamboo pole.

Breeding silkworms

In the village of Na Tam, in Lai Chau province, the cycle of cloth-making moves as smoothly as a bobbin turning: after planting comes the harvest, after the harvest the spinning, weaving, dyeing, sewing and embroidering. Na Tam lies tucked among the green hills, beside a river full of dabbling ducks, and has about fifty large houses in all.

We pass through a little bamboo door into Lo Thi Vang's house. Here she sits weaving in the shade. She has two looms: one for hemp, the other for the panel of silk brocade which she will use to decorate her skirt. Nearby are her spinning wheels, cotton gin and vat of indigo. A freshly dyed skein of silk is still dripping.

The hemp is harvested in the fields surrounding the village. The silkworms are reared on racks inside the house, and the indigo for the dye and the mulberry trees – which provide food for the silkworms – are planted close by. All Lo Thi Vang needs are a few remnants of flowered cotton to use for decoration, and she will buy these at the market in Bin Lu.

We receive a warm welcome and are invited by the master of the house to share a glass of rice wine, a cup of strong green tea and a puff of tobacco which we smoke from a hookah. This is the traditional form of welcome common to all these small hill tribes and the ritual never varies.

Breeding silkworms

The story goes that one day a silkworm cocoon accidentally fell into a cup of tea which a Chinese princess was drinking. As the princess tried to extract it from her drink, the cocoon unravelled into silky thread.

Sericulture is closely associated with the cultivation of mulberry trees and originated in China. The silkworm is the larva, or caterpillar, of the silkmoth (*Bombyx mori*). During its short life (35 to 40 days), the silkworm sheds its skin four times, increasing from 1 millimetre at birth to 7 or 8 millimetres. Silkworms feed exclusively on the leaves of the mulberry tree (*Monus alba*), irrespective of where they are bred, whether in southern France, Madras, Japan or North Vietnam. After shedding its skin for the final time, and following a period of voracious feeding, the silkworm gradually loses its appetite and its body takes on the yellow hue of the silk: it is now ready to weave its cocoon and is transferred to a bed of twigs. The silkworm attaches itself to a twig using silk secretions and for five or six days continues to 'dribble' silk from two silk glands called spinnerets, tirelessly tracing a figure of eight. It secretes a thread between 800 and 1,500 metres long, building a silk wall around itself that gradually thickens and hardens until it totally conceals the silkworm. The silkworm has now become a chrysalis, which will metamorphose into the white silkmoth. A few cocoons are kept aside for breeding purposes, but most of the cocoons are harvested before they have a chance to hatch. The cocoons are then immersed in boiling water, killing the silkworm and loosening the thread, and then unwound using a small brush, which picks up the silk thread. Several strands are gathered into a single thread, wound into a skein, washed (a process known as degumming) and then dyed.

Lu and Lao clothing, Vietnam

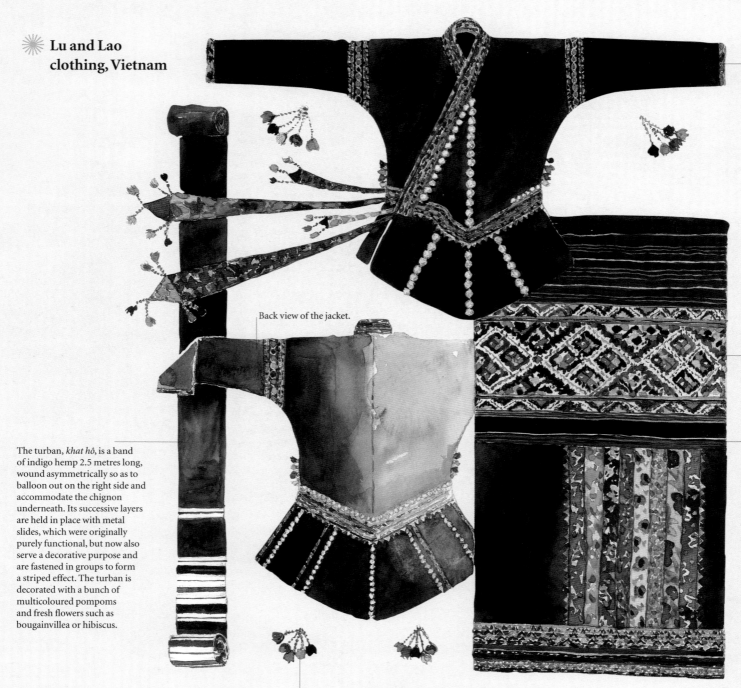

The long-line jacket in indigo hemp belies appearances and is in fact quite simple. It creates the effect of a fitted bodice by the clever use of braid: sewn at an angle the braid forms a point that accentuates the lower back. The collar is decorated with little squares set on their points. The belt follows a sinuous rather than a straight line and is made up of sections of flowered cotton with flaps at the end which serve to fasten the jacket. Rows of metal beads and pieces of stamped aluminium, alternating with silver coins, are used to conceal the seams, outline the neck and accentuate the flared look of the jacket body.

Back view of the jacket.

The brocade panel of the skirt.

The turban, *khat hô*, is a band of indigo hemp 2.5 metres long, wound asymmetrically so as to balloon out on the right side and accommodate the chignon underneath. Its successive layers are held in place with metal slides, which were originally purely functional, but now also serve a decorative purpose and are fastened in groups to form a striped effect. The turban is decorated with a bunch of multicoloured pompoms and fresh flowers such as bougainvillea or hibiscus.

The skirt is a rectangle 90 cm high and 110 cm wide, sewn like a tube and divided into two parts. Inserted between two striped sections at the top is a band of brocade, whose stepped and diamond motifs are woven using raw silk and multicoloured synthetic silk thread. The lower part of the skirt is decorated with eight vertical bands of flowered fabric sewn on to a plain base of indigo hemp, the flowered bands finished off with a row of cotton triangles with their edges folded under to form a row of 'teeth'.

Earrings are made of a range of attractive materials. On a silver base, gold- and silver-plated beads are threaded together, and finished with multicoloured pompoms. Courting girls add a bougainvillea flower to their left ear, and a silver torque called a *côn'g*. Women of all ages wear silver and copper bracelets.

Significant details

Tassels and pompoms *Yao decorations*

A Yao woman is inseparable from her pompoms. She sews them on everything. They are used to brighten up all indigo clothing, whether in tassel form, like the long strands of pink and magenta-coloured thread that escape from the neckline of a tunic, or in red wool, soft and bushy like a feather boa.

Red 'feather boa' pompoms

Hunting for pompoms is easy: they turn up almost daily on costumes, hats and bags, and are worn by every hill tribe. There are tiny pompoms, big round pompoms, long pompoms, fluffy pompoms. There are the individualists and the disciplined ranks, the festive garlands, red pompoms and pink ones and multicoloured ones, synthetic pompoms, pompoms made of cotton or wool, pompoms mingled with scraps of cloth… Ignoring frontiers, they sneak on to a coat collar in Muang Sing, Laos, latch on to a bag in Ha Giang, Vietnam, or adorn a baby's bonnet in Chiang Rai, Thailand. They are also commonly found decorating the front opening on an elegant Yao costume. Scattered down the neckline of a Red Yao tunic, they serve to highlight the cross-stitch designs, like grace notes in a musical score. Made of bushy red wool, they create the illusion of a fur collar on the indigo coat of a Yao woman from Laos.

The Lanten women's cotton tassels

Phuong and May are two young Lanten girls on their way to the market at Luang Namtha. Their plain tunics in plain indigo, their low-slung belts, the delicate finishings and the sophisticated accessories all give them a very contemporary look. A bag and white cotton leggings lighten the effect, and a hairpin, torque, earrings and silver buttons all add elegance to their outfit, and the long tassels of fuschia pink wool are the perfect finishing touch.

Left: Ly May Chan and Chao Tay May, two Yao Cham women, left their village early this morning to come and buy rice wine. The vendors are all Hmong and are clustered along the side of the track with jerry cans in front of them. The women sniff each can, take a sip, spit it out and exchange opinions.

 Yao Cham clothing, Vietnam

The tunic, *thô câm*, is made of plain indigo hemp and cut asymmetrically. It fastens under the right arm. The bias opening is trimmed with braid and the cuffs are decorated with red cotton and braid. The tunic has a decorative hem in flowered cotton. The neck fastening is a small silver claw-brooch from which streamers threaded with black and white beads hang, ending with silk and wool tassels. The trimmings form a chest piece around 50 cm long, which varies in style from village to village. One version may involve beads and multicoloured wool; another, magenta wool with no other additions; another may use pink cotton.

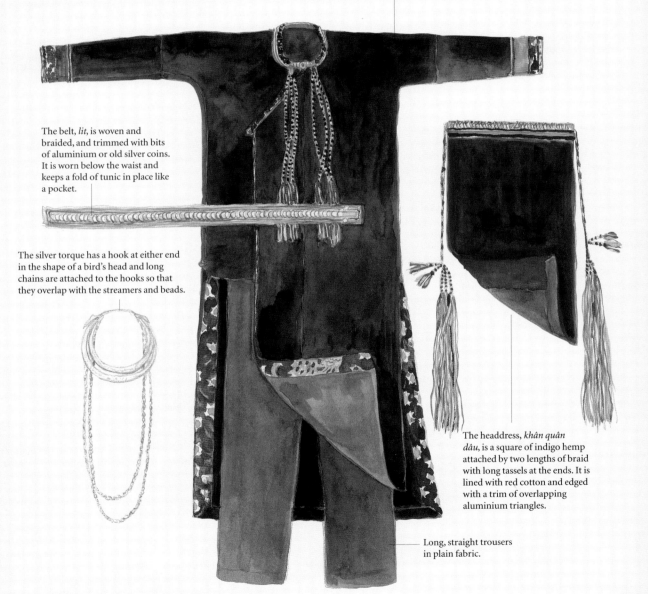

The belt, *lit*, is woven and braided, and trimmed with bits of aluminium or old silver coins. It is worn below the waist and keeps a fold of tunic in place like a pocket.

The silver torque has a hook at either end in the shape of a bird's head and long chains are attached to the hooks so that they overlap with the streamers and beads.

The headdress, *khân quân dâu*, is a square of indigo hemp attached by two lengths of braid with long tassels at the ends. It is lined with red cotton and edged with a trim of overlapping aluminium triangles.

Long, straight trousers in plain fabric.

Baskets and bags

Bags and baskets are an indispensable accessory for the men and women of South-East Asia. Worn across the body, a bag goes with them everywhere, whether they are working in the fields or shopping for groceries in the market.

Traditional costumes in South-East Asia rarely have pockets. Money tends to be secreted inside the folds of a garment and keys are carried on the end of a chain. The purpose of a bag is to carry any other objects that are needed as the wearers go about their daily business. This includes lunch, consisting of a ball of sticky rice wrapped in a banana leaf and some hot pickle; a pipe and tobacco for smokers; a betel nut, betel leaves and a piece of lime; an umbrella for protection against both the sun and the monsoon rains; a comb and safety pins. Men may also carry a small crossbow or a sling in case they spot a bird. A woman's bag will always contain some piece of embroidery in progress, some yarn, a spindle and a ball of cotton for spinning, and a skein of hemp for stripping. In the case of children, the bag will serve to carry their school things.

Bags are made of cloth and have a wide shoulder strap so that heavy objects can be carried without the strap digging into the wearer's shoulder.

Opposite: Two Flowered Hmong girls, seen from behind and recognizable by their pleated skirts decorated with batik and cross stitch embroidery, and their leggings with coloured ties.

In general, each hill tribe has its own bag to match its traditional costume. Like the clothes themselves, the bag is a badge of identity, indicating the community to which the wearer belongs. A pretty bag is also an advertisement for the skill of the woman who made it. Young girls take particular care over their first shopping bag, embroidering it and decorating it with pompoms, buttons, silver coins and beads, turning it into an accessory of the utmost sophistication, one that harmonizes with the rest of their outfit. In this respect, these South-East Asian girls are almost as preoccupied with fashion as their Western counterparts.

The Akha in Laos and the Red Yao in Vietnam still make their own bags today, but other groups tend to buy mass-produced ones in the markets or good old army-surplus holdalls. The same bag is then worn by a number of different communities. In its place, or in addition, a string bag is sometimes worn in the same fashion. Crocheted from hemp or with creepers gathered in the forest, and either dyed with indigo or left its natural colour, this kind of bag is useful for carrying shopping and also for fishing and hunting trips.

The path leading to a village is often narrow, so both men and women are obliged to carry supplies on their backs, in a woven basket equipped with two shoulder straps or a band worn around the head. Sometimes the basket is attached to a shaped plank which spreads the weight over the shoulders, so relieving the pressure on the forehead.

Xa Pho bag in hemp decorated with white seeds and embroidered motifs. Lung Phinh village, Sa Pa region.

Bag worn by the Lu and Lao women, demonstrating their weaving skills.

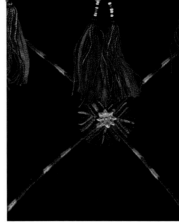

Nung bag, Sin Ho market.

Bag worn by the Giay, Black Yao and Tai and sold at all the markets.

Mass-produced bag, worn by the Hani and White Hmong. Striped cotton trimmed with embroidery.

Hemp bag, embroidered by a young Yao Cham girl. Quyet Tien market, Ha Giang region.

Red Yao bag, Sa Pa region.

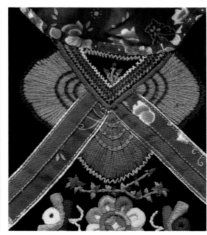

Red Yao bag in indigo hemp, embroidered with small cross-stitch motifs and trimmed with a red woollen fringe.

Yao purse.

White Trouser Yao pouch bag designed to hold betel nuts. It is worn on a silver chain.

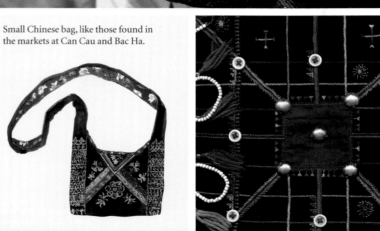

Small Chinese bag, like those found in the markets at Can Cau and Bac Ha.

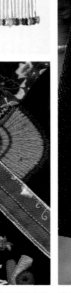

Yao Cham bag. Quyet Tien market, Ha Giang region. The bag can be worn over the shoulder or the strap can be re-attached to the bottom corners so that it can be worn as a backpack.

Giay, Vietnam

Lahu, Vietnam

Red Yao, Vietnam

Black Yao,
Vietnam

Flowered
Hmong,
Vietnam

Akha, Laos

All the trimmings

*In her striking headdress, Loa stands on the
road from Sa Pa to Phong Tho, in Vietnam.*

A love of accessories

She is wearing a pair of narrow-fitting trousers and
a long tunic decorated with red tassels. And all her
accessories are both beautiful and practical – even
the umbrella, an essential item in this wet climate,
which she carries in an elegant case over her
shoulder. Loa is almost as demanding as regards the
details and finishing of her accessories as a Western
customer buying luxury travel goods – except that
she is also extremely creative and resourceful. Her
most spectacular accessory is her hairpiece, the
traditional headdress of the Yao Lan Tien Sha.

Jewelry: a job for men

The mountain peoples of South-East Asia wear a
great deal of jewelry in beaten, chased and stamped
silver. Silvery metal is thought to represent light,
banish illness, help to keep the soul inside the body
and indicate social status. And it is not just the
women who wear the jewelry: men sporting
torques and bracelets are a common sight, and
children too wear jewelry, even though they may
be dressed in rags.

   Metal was once abundantly available in the
mines of China's Guizhou province, but today's
blacksmiths are obliged to melt down old coins –
colonial piastres and Chinese sapeks – or use nickel
silver, an alloy of copper, nickel and zinc. Families
have their own small foundries where the men work
during the period between two harvests. The tools
and skills are passed down from father to son,
and families sometimes build up large debts in
order to provide the necessary finery for their
daughters' weddings.

Left: Loa, seen here with her son
Pao Toa, earns a little money by
making children's hats, bags,
belts and bracelets and selling
them to passing tourists. She has
covered the silver ornament on
her headdress with plastic to
protect it from the rain.

Opposite, far right top: This
young Hmong girl from Mai
Chau, Vietnam, is wearing a
braided hairpiece and a double
pair of silver earrings.

Opposite, far right bottom:
A silver torque and a variety of
earrings: all these styles are worn
by several different hill tribes.

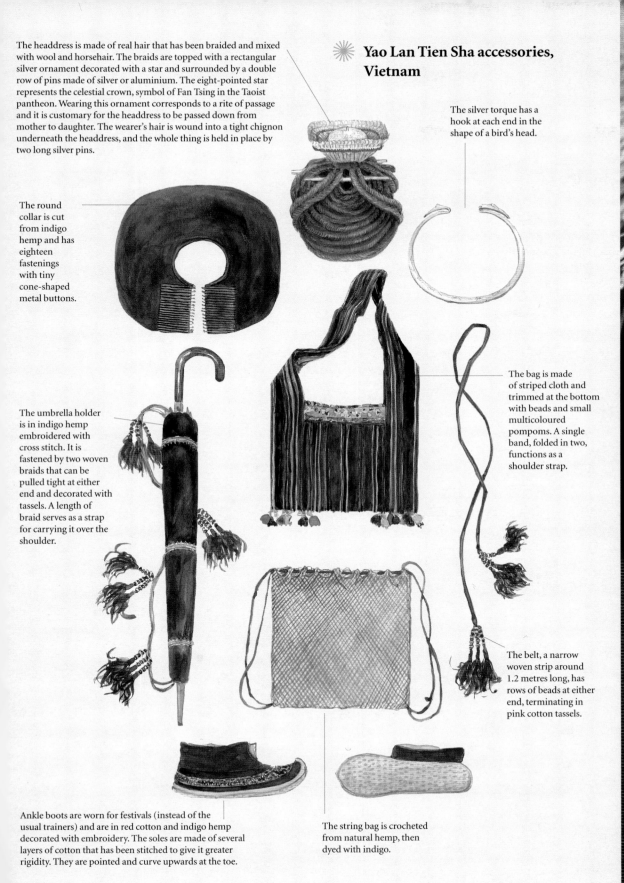

The headdress is made of real hair that has been braided and mixed with wool and horsehair. The braids are topped with a rectangular silver ornament decorated with a star and surrounded by a double row of pins made of silver or aluminium. The eight-pointed star represents the celestial crown, symbol of Fan Tsing in the Taoist pantheon. Wearing this ornament corresponds to a rite of passage and it is customary for the headdress to be passed down from mother to daughter. The wearer's hair is wound into a tight chignon underneath the headdress, and the whole thing is held in place by two long silver pins.

✳ Yao Lan Tien Sha accessories, Vietnam

The silver torque has a hook at each end in the shape of a bird's head.

The round collar is cut from indigo hemp and has eighteen fastenings with tiny cone-shaped metal buttons.

The umbrella holder is in indigo hemp embroidered with cross stitch. It is fastened by two woven braids that can be pulled tight at either end and decorated with tassels. A length of braid serves as a strap for carrying it over the shoulder.

The bag is made of striped cloth and trimmed at the bottom with beads and small multicoloured pompoms. A single band, folded in two, functions as a shoulder strap.

The belt, a narrow woven strip around 1.2 metres long, has rows of beads at either end, terminating in pink cotton tassels.

Ankle boots are worn for festivals (instead of the usual trainers) and are in red cotton and indigo hemp decorated with embroidery. The soles are made of several layers of cotton that has been stitched to give it greater rigidity. They are pointed and curve upwards at the toe.

The string bag is crocheted from natural hemp, then dyed with indigo.

Ethnic ornaments

Teeth lacquering is an ancient tradition that is now falling out of custom. Between Hanoi and Luang Prabang, however, it is still possible to meet a few old women whose dark-tinted smiles are a poignant reminder of the past.

'Lacquered teeth are as beautiful as the pips in an apple'

Wealthy mandarins are said to have dyed their teeth every evening. After dinner, a servant would bring a bowl of dye and a little stick: one end was pointed and used as a toothpick; the other was wrapped in a ball of cotton, which was dipped in the dye and rubbed on to the teeth.

A few mountain peoples, like the Lu, the Lao and the Akha, still lacquer their teeth with black dye. Others prefer to crown their teeth with gold or silver, an operation that fulfils several functions: it replaces unhealthy teeth, it looks good, and it's a symbol of social status and ethnic grouping.

Women's ornaments

Is there perhaps an analogy between the growing Western taste for body piercing and modification, and the spectacular body ornaments worn by Padaung and Bre women? Is this a case of aesthetic mimesis or a worldwide impulse to be different? The cultural contexts are not the same, of course: the Karen women may experience a pressure to affirm their identity, but in the West body piercing and tattoos are generally a personal choice.

The famous Paduang or 'giraffe women' are Burmese Karen refugees living in Thailand, resettled in villages where they scrape a living from tourism and the sale of handicrafts. A Padaung girl's metamorphosis begins at the age of 5, when she dons her first copper neck ring following the application of an ointment of royal jelly, grease and coconut milk to her skin. Another ring will be added each year until she marries and she will wear a little cotton cushion decorated with beads and pompoms under her chin to prevent the rings from rubbing.

The Bre women are also a sub-group of the Karen, and are known locally as the 'big ears' on account of their distended earlobes. Their clothes are almost a visual irrelevance: what instantly draws the eye is their profusion of jewelry – the huge silver rings filled with a blue stone that stretch their ears, the bands of copper around their ankles and knees, and the chain necklaces decorated with old Indian rupees, Burmese coins dating from the time when the country was a British colony, glass beads and silver crescents – as if each Bre woman were an ideogram representing the history of her people.

Above: A Padaung girl from the village of Ban Ya Pa, in Thailand. Young women's accessories combine precious materials, such as silver and copper, with beads made of paste and glass, plastic bracelets and synthetic cloth (for the headdress).

Opposite, above left: Like Padaung women, Bre women wear copper rings and glass beads round their knees and ankles.

Opposite, below left: This Lahu Shi woman from Thailand is wearing extravagant silver earrings. Her black cotton jacket is delicately trimmed with bands of cotton appliqué and little silver balls sewn together in triangles.

This White Trouser Yao woman from the Viet Quang region of Vietnam describes how she lacquers her teeth:

'I make the dye paste by crushing ants' wings in lemon juice and letting the mixture steep for seven days. Then I spread the paste on an areca leaf and apply it to my teeth using a bit of burnt coconut shell. I do it at night and repeat the process at least five times, until my teeth are really black. In the meantime, I can't eat anything solid. I just drink. The colour fades gradually, so I do the whole thing again every year and help to keep it going by chewing betel. The dye stops your teeth decaying.'

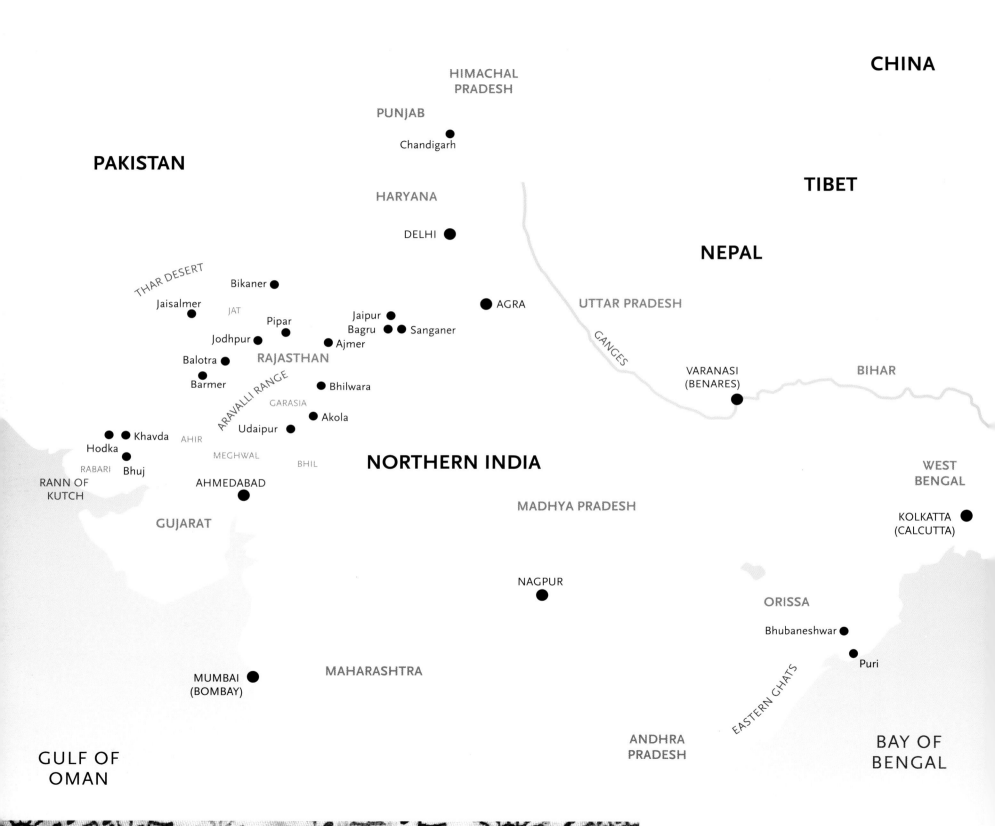

Orissa, Rajasthan, Gujarat
The colours of India

'Less is more,' comments Ashok, nodding his head and adjusting his *lunghi*. The people one meets travelling across northern India are strikingly well dressed, although the beauty of their clothing boils down to a simple rectangle of cloth: a draped sari for the women, a *dhoti* or *lunghi* for the men.

A rectangle of cloth, but not any old cloth. The simpler the garment, the more special the fabric needs to be. And a variety of techniques are used to embellish it, including brocade work, the addition of gold thread, ikat threads, sequins and mirrors, embroidering and patterning using dyes, knotting and block-printing.

The simplicity of the sari contrasts with the unbelievable richness of clothing styles in northern India, the meeting place of Hindu culture and the Mughal dynasties.

The Mughal invaders brought their own tailors and dressmakers, and with a snip of their scissors and a few lengths of thread, cashmeres, silks and muslins were transformed into Rajput jackets, Turkoman trousers, generous pleated skirts, cropped bodices, embroidered gilets and long tunics. To discover this rich heritage, we have to cross the Indian subcontinent, penetrating the snowy wastes of Himachal Pradesh and passing through the valleys of Manali and Kullu, land of the *pashmina*; travel across the Rann of Kutch in search of the mirrorwork embroiderers, discover the silk workers of Bangalore; enter the workshops of Ahmedabad, and seek out the cashmere embroiderers in the streets of Srinagar; visit the master weavers of Orissa and Andhra Pradesh, and the dyers of Jaipur. India is one massive harvesting, spinning, weaving, embroidering and printing operation, consuming and exporting vast quantities of cloth both at the local craft level and on a mass-produced scale. There is nothing that India cannot produce, and everything has influenced the fashions of the West.

The fashion for Indian fabrics was being reported as early as 1672, in a French journal called *Le Mercure galant*, when Europe was already importing cashmeres from Hindustan, handkerchiefs from Madras and silks and chintzes from the Coromandel Coast. Western designers, ranging from Paul Poiret to Kenzo and Dries Van Noten, have long drawn inspiration from India's great textile resources. Think of floral Laura Ashley skirts and the Empress Josephine's palm-leaf shawls; think of the tie-dye tunics and kaftans of the sixties and seventies.

From the state of Orissa, in Gujarat, the kingdom of mirrors, our journey takes us through Rajasthan and to the Rann of Kutch.

Indian prints

In the cotton fields

Evening is falling over the Rajasthani countryside. The sky is a blaze of colour, criss-crossed by the flight patterns of green bee-eaters. At a bend in the road, we suddenly come across a cotton plantation where a group of women are finishing off their harvest, scattered across the field like so many brilliant flowers.

Here, then, is the raw material in its natural state: fluffy, snow-white balls of growing cotton. India and cotton are as interwoven as tangled threads. Cotton, a semi-tropical plant that grows on 'black ground', is cultivated, spun and woven throughout the subcontinent and entered the pages of history the day that Gandhi encouraged his people to boycott British textiles, so elevating the status of homespun cotton or *khadi*. Cotton brought India prosperity, but Indian women now have a passion for synthetic fibres – which are lighter, more economical and more hardwearing – so the future of cotton is uncertain.

Cotton is produced on a modest scale in Rajasthan, supplying the region's small cotton mills and sufficing for local consumption. Depending on its quality, it is used to make carpets, cotton cloth, net or muslin. Cotton for saris and veils (*odhni*) needs to be very fine, like *malmal* from Mathania, near Jodhpur, whereas skirts (*ghaghara* or *ghagra*), cropped blouses (*choli*), tunics (*kurta*) and trousers (*salwar*) are cut from thicker cotton. Cotton that has been ginned and carded is also used to stuff mattresses and pillows and make bedcovers and padded clothing in the purest Mughal tradition.

The amount Surya is paid will depend on how much cotton she picks.

Previous pages, left: The skirt that this woman is holding is cut from a length of black wool patterned with white checks and hemmed with embroidery and inlaid mirrors.

Previous pages, right: Lengths of cloth drying in the yard at a Balotra workshop.

Opposite: Lakshmi, Sunita, Amitabh and Surya, bundling up cotton ready for weighing.

Block printing *The skirts of Rajasthan*

The workshop is silent but for the dull thump as the printer bangs down the wooden stamp twice in succession. The evening light is slanting into the dark room. Stretched the length of the felt-topped table, the cloth lifts slightly in the breeze from the fan. The **chhipa walla***'s hand travels back and forth between the cart laden with pigments and the cloth with its rows of motifs. He selects another block, and a different colour, and goes over the design, taking great care to line up the motifs exactly, carrying on in this vein until he has printed the whole cloth in a range of different colours.*

Generation of printers have repeated this same painstaking process. Generations have watched those printed cotton skirts swinging rhythmically against the ankles of a beautiful Indian girl.

The beautiful woman, in this case, is Heera, whose name in Marwari, the dialect of the Barmer region, means 'diamond'. In this desert landscape, standing near the pool of grey rainwater, she looks more like a ruby – wrapped in her red veil, and decked in her red bracelets and printed skirt.

She has brought her small herd here, frightening away the birds that gather to drink – the demoiselle cranes, the grey francolins and the peacock.

Left: A peasant woman wearing the pomegranate print skirt from Akola.

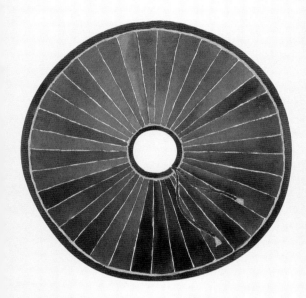

Above: The beauty of the Rajasthani tribal skirt is its fullness and the graceful way it swings as the wearer moves. This particular skirt is made up of thirty-six trapezoid-shaped panels. It fits closely at the waist and widens out to form a bell shape 9 metres in circumference. The bias-cut hem in bright red cotton has been added on and is accentuated by a second narrow band in yellow cotton, also cut on the bias. A belt in the same red cotton overlaps the waistband and is fastened by drawstring ties. The skirt panels have been cut head to tail to keep wastage to a minimum, and as a result the direction of the pattern alternates from one panel to the next. The panels are 75 cm long, barely 10 cm wide at the waist and 25 cm wide at the hem, and the whole skirt requires more than 6 metres of fabric!

Above: With her *dantli* (sickle) in her hand, Sunita, a Rabari woman from the Pachpadra region, has neatly folded up her *ghaghara* skirt to work in the fields. She wears a *kanchali*, a close-fitting bodice that leaves her stomach bare, and two *odhni* or shawls: one over her head, and the other around her waist, to be used for carrying the millet she is harvesting. She wears plastic and silver bracelets on both her wrists and her upper arms, right up to her shoulders, and silver ankle bracelets adorn her legs.

Leaning on her stick for support, Heera is keeping an eye on her small herd. Hanging from the belt of her skirt (*ghaghara*) are a number of charms, along with the keys to the metal trunks where she keeps her trousseau and her provisions. We talk to her and learn that her husband is an opium addict and no longer leaves his bed, his *charpoy*. Heera has to manage the home and look after their three children entirely on her own.

Her skirt, called a *ghaghara* or *ghagra*, is decorated with the traditional *katar* pattern – a white dagger motif produced by resist-dyeing, framed by stripes – on an indigo ground. It turns out that the skirt is made of printed synthetic jersey rather than cotton. I am a little disappointed, but Heera explains: 'I don't have any choice. The synthetic material is half the price of the printed cotton I used to buy in Balotra. The skirt lasts three years, dries in no time, and doesn't fade in the sun.' The choice is very clear.

The skills of the *chhipa walla*, the master dyers, go back generations. Alongside the traditional workshops, other small businesses have grown up, quick to respond to the demands of rural communities for synthetic versions of traditional print fabrics.

Natural dyes

Indigo is obtained by a cold fermentation process in which leaves from the indigo plant are macerated with lime and molasses.

Madder root produces red, brown and purple.

Yellow is made with turmeric roots or pomegranate skins.

Black is obtained by macerating pieces of scrap iron (such as horseshoes) for about twenty days in water and molasses until fermentation occurs. The solution is then thickened with a paste of crushed tamarind seeds.

Green is produced when yellow dye – obtained from boiled pomegranate skins and turmeric – is overprinted on a base of indigo.

Crushed tamarind seeds boiled in water and mixed with starch and madder produce a whole range of browns when iron sulphate is added to dyes made of henna, gambier, onion skin or safflower.

Above: The Akola workshop. Before printing, men beat the fabric to soften it.

Top of page: A range of natural dyes and a printing block.

Yaseen, a printer and dyer

Block printing used to be done in small workshops all over Rajasthan, but today the main centres for this type of textile printing are Jaipur, Sanganer, Bagru, Chittorgarh, near Udaipur, and Balotra, between Jodhpur and Barmer. Yaseen is the only traditional printer and dyer left in his town.

'For ten generations our family have been dyeing and printing cotton to make skirts for the local women,' explains the friendly Yaseen, who is a Muslim. 'At one time, there was a whole *chhipa walla* community operating all along the river, but we are the only family business still going since the arrival of modern printing techniques. We are lucky enough to be working for the Anglo-Indian company Anokhi, producing handmade cloth for export. I buy my raw cotton in twenty-metre lengths from the Mewar Mills at Bhilwara.'

Above: A design in three sections, block printed on an 8-metre roll of fabric at the Akola workshops. A Muslim woman will get her tailor to cut trousers (*salwar*), a tunic (*kameez*) and a long veil (*dupatta*) from the same cloth to make an elegantly coordinated outfit. Since all three garments are cut from a single piece of printed fabric, they will match one another perfectly, with the only difference being in the stamped motifs.

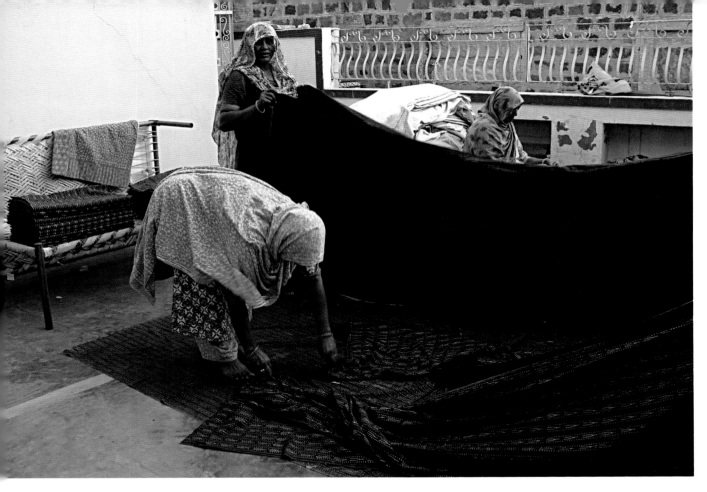

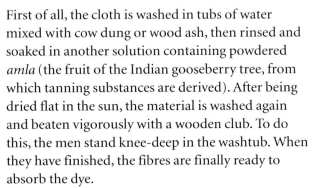

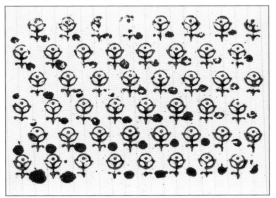

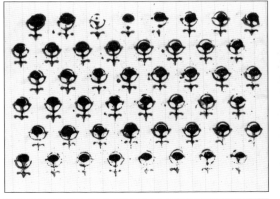

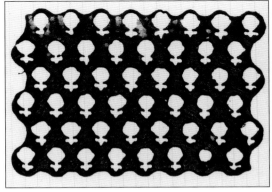

First of all, the cloth is washed in tubs of water mixed with cow dung or wood ash, then rinsed and soaked in another solution containing powdered *amla* (the fruit of the Indian gooseberry tree, from which tanning substances are derived). After being dried flat in the sun, the material is washed again and beaten vigorously with a wooden club. To do this, the men stand knee-deep in the washtub. When they have finished, the fibres are finally ready to absorb the dye.

'I do use chemical colorants too, of course, but I make it a point of honour to stick to natural dyes for certain customers,' says Yaseen, as he explains the range of vegetable pigments available.

Above: The day's work is almost over for these Muslim women in Balotra. Dressed in their *salwar kameez* and their *odhni*, they are folding cotton saris that have been drying in the yard and are piling them neatly on the *charpoy* in the corner (above right).

Right: Three block-printed versions of the same design.

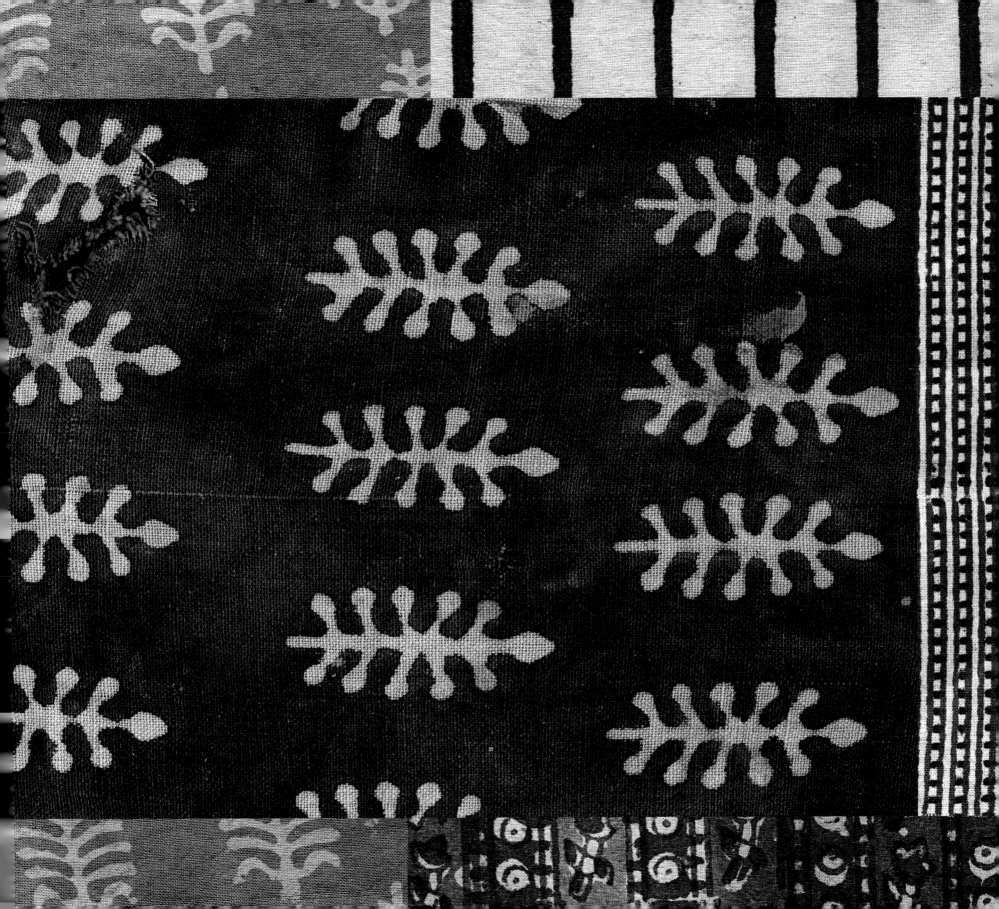

Previous pages: Examples of block-print designs from the workshops at Balotra, Akola and Pipar. Some use a single colour, others two or three.

Opposite: A peasant woman with her cow. She is wearing a pomegranate print skirt from Akola.

Top and centre: A printing block or *thappa*. It is made from a piece of teak delicately carved by a carpenter, or *khati*, who uses fine gouges to cut the design.

Above: A woman in a *bandhani* skirt with a fine pattern of dots.

Suresh's pomegranate prints

These days, the only people who buy clothes in block-printed cotton are women from rural communities, a handful of sophisticated Indians living in Delhi, and Westerners holidaying in Jaipur. The majority of Indian women prefer synthetic fabrics because of their brilliant colours and their lightness, and their shining lurex threads, although such fabrics can also be highly flammable.

'She is a Jat,' my guide, Prakash, tells me as he points out a local woman. 'And over there is a Kalbeliya, a gypsy, linked to the blacksmith caste who travel from village to village.' Her skirt, or *ghaghara*, is tied below her navel, and her short blouse, or *choli*, comes to just below her breasts, so that her hips and midriff are exposed – like those of a young Western woman in her cropped top and low-slung jeans.

The design and colour of a woman's skirt are an immediate clue to her identity. 'That woman is a Mina. She is a member of the Bhil community and her skirt comes from the Akola *chhipa walla* workshop. Let's go and see it,' suggests Prakash.

The dusty road winds its way between acacia trees. After several kilometres, it brings us to a broad sandy area carpeted with a mosaic of red and blue rectangles. There is a pool of stagnant water nearby and it almost looks as if the few browsing cattle are grazing on the cloth itself. The sun is beating down, but this place has a lunar feel about it. The sand is spangled with blue pools and threads of every hue, and the scraggy bushes are decked in scraps of cloth that have got caught on their spines.

Suresh, the local *chhipa walla*, suddenly looms into view, larger than life. Suresh's workshops produce a rustic cloth printed with stylized red pomegranates on an indigo ground. It takes six metres of this fabric to make the *ghaghara* worn

by local tribeswomen, explains Suresh, and he points at the swirling skirts of a villager who is walking past, barefoot, her ankles decorated with heavy silver rings. After the cloth has been washed, it is then mordanted, which means that the red, alizarin-based dye is fixed by treating the areas to be printed with alum. The cloth is washed again. The red patterns are now fixed. Both they and the areas to be kept white are masked with clay, using the dye-resist technique known as *dhabu* in Hindi, and the cloth is then immersed in a vat of indigo before being over-dyed in black.

The cloth is washed and dried for the third and last time, at which point the powdery, dry mud brushes off to reveal the beautiful red of the pomegranate motifs underneath.

'We print much better things,' boasts Suresh and he spreads out a number of saris and light, airy veils, printed on a cloth with a silk weft and cotton warp, and a selvedge of gold threads known as *garbhi*. He unfolds a beautiful block-printed *khadi* fabric and another block-printed fabric, *tussar*, then takes us into the workshop where a printer is stamping gold motifs on a piece of black cloth. 'We prepare a paste made of gum, *roghan*, mixed with powdered gold or silver leaf, and we use a small copper stamp,' explains Suresh. The technique is a cost-saving alternative to embroidering with gold thread: 'It sparkles but it's cheap,' he says.

Silkscreen prints from Sanganer

Sanganer, just outside Jaipur, has long been a centre for textile printing thanks to the proximity of the Dhundnadi River, whose mineral-rich waters are used to give the dye colours a particular brilliance. Unfortunately, the river is now badly polluted by chemical effluents.

A few block-printing workshops are still to be found in the *chhipa basti*, the printers' and dyers' quarter, but Sanganer is known today for its production of cheap silkscreen prints used to make household linen and saris for everyday wear.

Silkscreen printing uses a wooden frame with silk or organdie stretched across it to form a screen. Areas of the screen are masked off and the printing ink is poured into the frame and spread over the screen with a rubber squeegee. The ink penetrates the silk fibres and prints the fabric that is spread beneath it on a long table. Two men, working opposite one another, manipulate the frame, lifting it clear and repositioning it so the design can be repeated along the whole length of cloth. Using another screen, a second and sometimes a third colour can be printed onto the masked-off sections. Silkscreen printing is less sophisticated but quicker than block printing and, being a manual technique, it creates imperfections which are also part of its charm.

Previous pages: Lengths of pomegranate print cloth drying by the river at Akola.

Above left: This camel driver is collecting a pile of wet cloths. The camels used for this kind of work are neatly shorn and tattooed with their owners' initials.

Above centre: Women employed to spread saris and tablecloths on the banks of the river at Sanganer. Their veils protect them from the sun and also from sand whipped up by the wind.

Above right: These lengths of cloth have been steamed and washed and are now drying on tall bamboo racks. When they are ready, they will be folded and delivered to the silkscreen workshops.

Opposite: Lengths of saffron-coloured cotton due to be printed with a black design in the Sanganer workshops.

In Sanganer, every small courtyard, every single nook and cranny, has been transformed into a drying area where lengths of printed cloth are suspended on wires. The silkscreens, which can measure up to 1.5 by 2 metres, are washed down and stacked, making the town ressemble an artist's studio full of blank canvases.

Mr Doraya gives tourists a tour of his workshop, at Laxmi Colony, before taking them to visit his shop, a place that is piled high with quilted bedcovers, household linen, shawls and saris. I am astonished at the cornucopia emanating from such a modest workshop. Seeing the expression on my face, he says: 'Come. I will show you' and takes me to the riverbank. Here, between willows and bamboos, in a row of open-air workshops, an army of men and women (most of them Muslim) are washing, dyeing, stretching, folding long lengths of cloth in an incessant hum of activity, punctuated by the cawing of crows or the roar of a camel.

The camel is an important part of any workshop staff. Harnessed to a cart loaded high with streaming tablecloths and saris, it makes its way slowly along the riverbank, stopping to let the women unload the cargo and spread it across the burning sand, not far from where the rinsing tubs and dye vats and tall drying racks are set up.

A number of Western textile designers owe their inspiration to silkscreen prints. The first fabrics designed in 1911 by Raoul Dufy for the Ateliers de Paul Poiret, Sonia Delaunay's 'simultaneous' fabrics, the prints of the Wiener Werkstätte and the huge flowers created by Maija Isola for Marimekko in the 1960s, all started life in Scandinavian, Parisian and Viennese silkscreen workshops not unlike those of Sanganer.

Mud and indigo *A chhipa walla at work*

Indigo runs like a refrain through the pages of this book. Skilfully obtained from green leaves, it conjures up that deepest of blues, the blue of the ocean, and the blue of the sky as it lies reflected in the dye vats of Asia, of Africa, of America – and right here in the heart of Rajasthan.

My guide, Prakash, has warned me that we will have trouble finding a workshop open in Pipar at the end of Ramadan. Indigo dyeing is a job generally done by Muslims, since Hindus regard it as impure because of the fermentation involved. And, sure enough, the village is really quiet. One *chhipa walla*, however, is busy working. His name is Abdul.

Abdul's workshop is by the river, the perfect location, since he needs water for rinsing his dyes and open areas for drying his cloth, and the clay deposits he collects from the river bed are ideal for dye-resist printing.

Abdul speaks no English and has to explain with gestures, but given his obvious technical expertise and the precision of his movements, words are redundant anyway.

After washing the cloth (see page 75), he spreads it over a low table covered with felt and, sitting on a small cushion on the ground, stamps out his patterns, dipping his wooden block, or *thappa*, in a tub of liquid mud placed to his right and applying it to the cloth with a firm pressure. The trickiest part of the exercise is getting the patterns to line up exactly. When the printed design is dry, Abdul stirs his dye vat, an earthenware jar half buried in the ground, with a stick to oxygenate the contents, then gently immerses the cloth in the mixture.

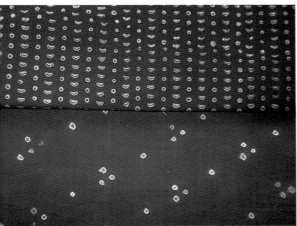

Abdul holding up a piece of cloth printed with a number of different designs.

Top left: An indigo vat and an indigo plant.

Centre left: Lengths of indigo cloth drying in the sun.

Bottom left and top centre: The traditional pomegranate design, representing the fruit in stylized form.

Above: Pipar is a blue town, like Jodhpur. Indigo dye is diluted and painted on the walls of the houses.

Indigo dyeing – whether a natural or synthetic pigment is used – is a cold-water process involving immersion in a dye solution to which molasses and lime have been added to accelerate fermentation.

After soaking, the cloth is pale yellowish green. It turns blue on contact with the air, and a darker blue is obtained by repeated immersion. As the mud dries, it cracks and crumbles to powder, revealing the pattern in negative, white on a blue ground.

Abdul's final task is to add other colours by block printing over the top of the white motifs.

Above: Abdul Hamid, a *chhipa walla* from Pipar, begins the first stage of the printing process. He uses clay to print his cloth using the dye-resist method. He dips his wooden stamp into a mixtu[re] of river mud, gum Arabic and lime, known as *dhabu*, and scatters sand over the stamped patterns to absorb the excess moisture and accelerate the drying process. He then soaks the cloth in a vat of indigo. When the mud mixture is washed off, the stylized flowers will appear in white resist on a deep blue ground.

Left: Abdul with his vat of indigo. He explains: *'Dyers, like blacksmiths, are sometimes former Untouchables who have converted to Islam in order to escape the caste system.'*

Below left: Cloth stamped with *dhabu*. Abdul holds it up to show how the white parts have absorbed the indigo and the parts that were stamped with mud are still white.

Below: Indigo cloth drying in a yard.

 Stars, stripes and mirrors

Cotton saris *The ikat technique in Orissa*

Orissa's sandy coastline is lapped by the waters of the Bay of Bengal. It is a favourite holiday destination for the people of Calcutta, and also a pilgrimage site for Bengalis, who flock here in great numbers to visit the Temple of Puri dedicated to Lord Jagannath and the Temple of the Sun at Konarak. Few tourists, however, venture into this eastern corner of India, home to its aboriginal or Dravidian peoples, the Khond, the Santal, the Bonda and the Gadaba.

Orissa is also the India of traditional fishermen, rice planters and artisans, like the weavers of cotton cloth and silk voile, and of garments like the lunghi, *the* dupatta *and the* odhni, *which clothe millions of Indians on a daily basis.*

There are no fewer than 40,000 looms to be found in the districts surrounding Bhubaneshwar, Sambalpur, Nuapatna, Bargarh and Balangir. In every village, behind every mud wall decorated with *manadasa* (patterns made of rice meal), spinning wheels hum and shuttles click to and fro.

Avinesh weaves saris in Sonepur. Once his mattress has been rolled up in the morning, his bedroom becomes his workshop. There is a hollow about 50 centimetres deep in the beaten earth floor beneath his loom. He sits on the floor, on a small pile of rags, with his feet in the hollow, operating the pedals. The particular speciality of Orissa weavers like Avinesh is the ikat technique, used for decorating silk and cotton saris. Like a navigator who plots his position on a map of the oceans, checking where parallels and meridians intersect, Avinesh sits at his loom crossing his resist-dyed warp and weft threads to create a 'double ikat'.

Ikat is a method of dyeing where the threads are bound tightly before they are dyed and woven. They can be intertwined in such a way as to form a variety of patterns – geometric shapes, squares, rectangles, stars and crosses – whose contours may be slightly blurred depending on the rigidity of the warp and weft threads and the uneven penetration of the dye beneath the ties. The resulting weave is very subtle, often in two colours only, its beauty increased by the randomly blurred effects, It has served as inspiration for Rakesh Thakore and many other textile designers.

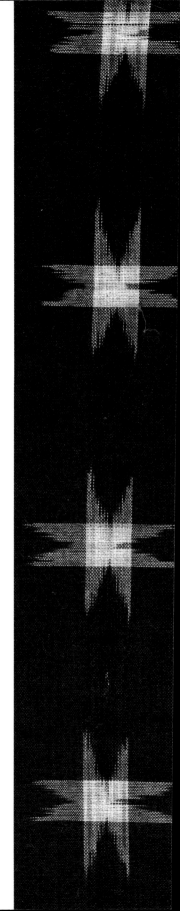

Above, top: Sita has just coated this adobe wall in clay and is decorating it with motifs symbolizing wealth and fertility: grains of rice, sheaves of millet, and turkeys.

Above, bottom: Lala is standing in front of the Baidyanathi Banyan, wearing a sari in red, black and white cotton printed with a traditional design from Saktapar, a double ikat in which both warp and weft threads have been tie-dyed to form a pattern of squares. She has just wriggled through the sacred banyan's hanging roots – a custom she believes will bring her good luck.

Above: These fishermen's caps and shirts complement their *lunghi* skirts, which are made from rectangles of dyed cotton. The checked designs are ikat.

Right: A village dressmaker's sign. On offer are made-to-measure garments such as the *choli*, a short fitted blouse, and the *pavada*, a kind of petticoat worn by Hindu women beneath their saris.

Surita sells fish, walking up and down the beach at Puri. The little cushion on top of her head helps her to balance the basket in which she carries her fish and her set of scales.

The secrets of ikat are known to two communities, the Mehers and the Patras. Hindus will work equally happily with either cotton or silk, but Buddhists will only work with cotton because silk production involves killing the silkworms, which is against Buddhist teachings.

As well as saris, Orissa's weavers produce loincloths, or *lunghi*, which can also sometimes double as scarves and towels, as well as lengths of ikat and decorative fabrics for the home.

A full description of the ikat technique – which is thought to have originated in Malaysia – is given in the chapter on Guatemalan *jaspe* (see page 130).

A sari is just a simple rectangle of cloth, but it comes to life when it is worn and draped. An Indian woman will choose her sari with care and wrap it in a number of different ways depending on the customs of her community. At Puri, on the Bay of Bengal, it is fascinating to watch women wading out into the sea, determined to enjoy the water and waves, still fully clothed in their saris.

Saris, veils and turbans *Tie-dye, or* bandhani

We are in a street in the Muslim quarter of Jodhpur, near Merti Gate. Food is being prepared in the house, ready for the festival of Eid ul Adha, but out here on the terrace Sherbano is doing a different job, her fingers moving deftly back and forth as she hums a Bollywood love song to herself. She is tying cotton scarves according to a design marked out in pencil on the white cloth, making thousands of little knots round a nakhaliyo, a metal thimble shaped like a fingernail, which she is wearing on her index finger. When the work is finished, it will be collected from her and taken to the dyers.

The technique Sherbano is using is practised throughout the world. It is known as chunidar *in Rajasthan,* shibori *in Japan* and plangi *in Indonesia, and to us as tie-dye. The English word 'bandanna' – used to refer to cowboy-style neckerchiefs, often with a white pattern on a red or blue ground – dates back to the 18th-century fashion for Indian* bandhani. *In the 1960s and 1970s, tie-dye clothing was all the rage among the hippies, symbolizing a subversive attitude to fashion that cocked a snook at the middle classes and their conservative styles of dress.*

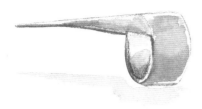

Above and right: The *nakhaliyo* is a pointed thimble worn on the index finger to help in the tying of very small knots.

Below: *Lehariya*: cloth rolled and tied on the bias.

'Since I only get paid ten rupees for every square I tie, I can assure you that I don't stop for a minute,' says Sherbano with a smile – but she has taken the time to decorate her feet with henna (*mehndi*) for the festival of Eid.

Methods of tying: *chunidar*, *lehariya* and *mothara*

Each of these mysterious names refers to a different method of tying. Whether the tying is done at random intervals, on the diagonal, criss-cross, or zig-zag, and whether the patterns are arabesques, scattered dots, waves or checks, all these techniques are based on the same principle: they all involve folding, tying and sewing a section of cloth so that when it is soaked in the dye, the tied area will not absorb the colour and will appear instead as a negative pattern on a coloured ground. The opposite process then follows, whereby the coloured section of cloth is isolated with a plastic film and the white section is soaked in a dye bath. This process of isolating sections of cloth and dyeing the rest can be repeated several times in order to produce a wide spectrum of colours. What is crucial is that the cloth should be very fine and highly permeable.

An artisan from Jaipur

The Patnis in Jaipur are Hindus and the craft of the *bandhani walla* is passed on from father to son. Arpit has taken over from his father Arun, who talks politics, sitting in his workshop in Johari Bazar. Arpit is fussy about his choice of fabrics. He gets his supplies of cotton voile from the neighbouring town of Bhilwara, but goes to Bangalore and

Left: The roofs of Jodhpur.
Right: 'Kite' pattern in tie-dye.

China to buy silk georgette and silk chiffon, and to Germany for his synthetic dyes. The fabrics are distributed to home workers, who do the tying, and are collected again and returned to the workshop, where Arpit supervises the dyeing process. The first step is to treat the cloth with acid to make it more absorbent. The cloth is then dyed in one of a range of pots of colour bubbling away on small gas burners, rinsed, dried, and dyed a second and a third time. The whole thing is a carefully orchestrated operation, and the walls of Arpit's shop are lined with piles of wedding saris, rows of veils (*odhni*), and lengths of cloth designed to be wound into turbans (*pagri*). 'To show that they are the genuine article, and not just machine-prints, my *bandhani* are sold with the ties in place. I only untie one end of a shawl, so the customer can see the design,' explains Arpit. 'Three-quarters of the cloth I produce stays in India; the rest goes to Saudi Arabia. I'd be better off if I were a jeweller, like my friends, but I love my job.'

A dye-worker in Jodhpur. Her son dyes the fabrics over a gas burner and she rinses them in her copper basin. She works for a range of customers – a woman bringing in a sari that needs freshening up; a man depositing a pair of faded trousers. In a flash, the clothes are transformed and the water runs off in the open gully, coloured with a rainbow of chemical dyes.

'Your dreams, our designs'

Another very popular tie-dye technique is *lehariya*, a word that means 'waves' in Hindi and evokes the monsoon rains. The old quarter of Jodhpur is lined with *havelis*, one-time private homes that have now been partially transformed into workshops where the *rangari walla* or *rangrez walla*, the dyers, the masters of colour (*rang* in Hindi) run their family businesses. 'Your dreams, our designs' is the slogan devised by Salman and Hakim, two brothers who have set up their workshop in a ramshackle *haveli* overlooking the old town. The cloth is rinsed in the fountain in the yard, wrapped up by the brothers' young assistants – who are forever in the process of tying or untying – and immersed in dye baths on the roof terrace.

The length of fabric destined to become a sari or a turban is rolled diagonally from one corner to the opposite edge, then tied at regular intervals and dyed. Salman undoes the ties and shows us the diagonal stripes. Once the cloth is dry, it is rolled up again and retied, this time on the other diagonal, and re-dyed. The resulting check pattern is known as *mothara*, 'because the spaces inbetween are the size of a lentil, the word for which is *moth* in Hindi,' he explains. 'It's a technique used for turbans.' Another technique involves pleating the fabric lengthwise to produce a chevron pattern that is popular in southern Rajasthan: it is called *bhopal shahi*, after its creator, Maharana Bhopal Singh.

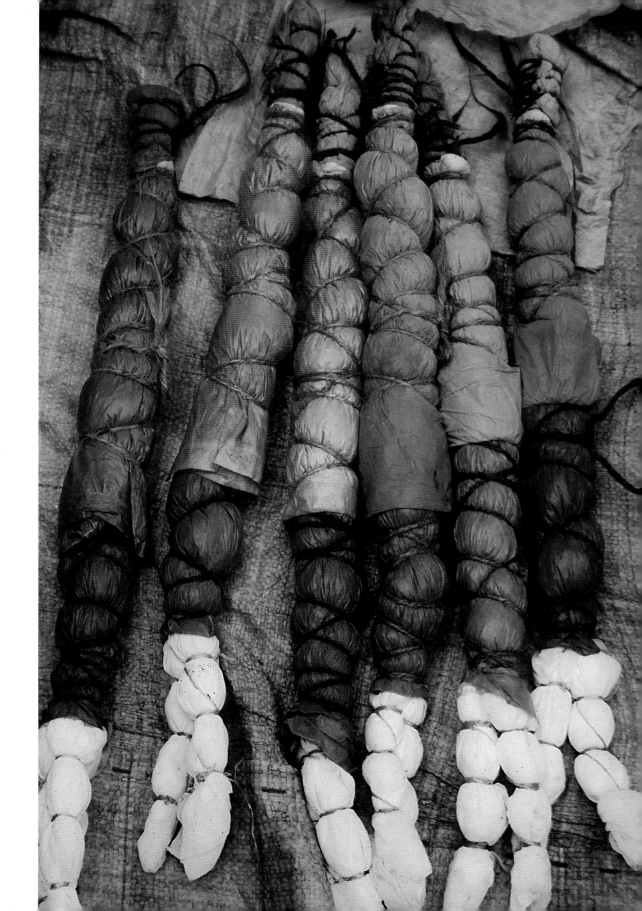

Below, top row: In Jodhpur's *rangari* dye workshops.
Below, bottom left: These fat wands wrapped in coloured plastic are shawls that have been tied in Jaipur.
Bottom centre: *Bandhani* being removed from an initial dye bath.
Bottom right: This turban is a splendid example of the *mothara* technique.
Opposite: A length of undyed cloth that has been tied prior to dyeing.

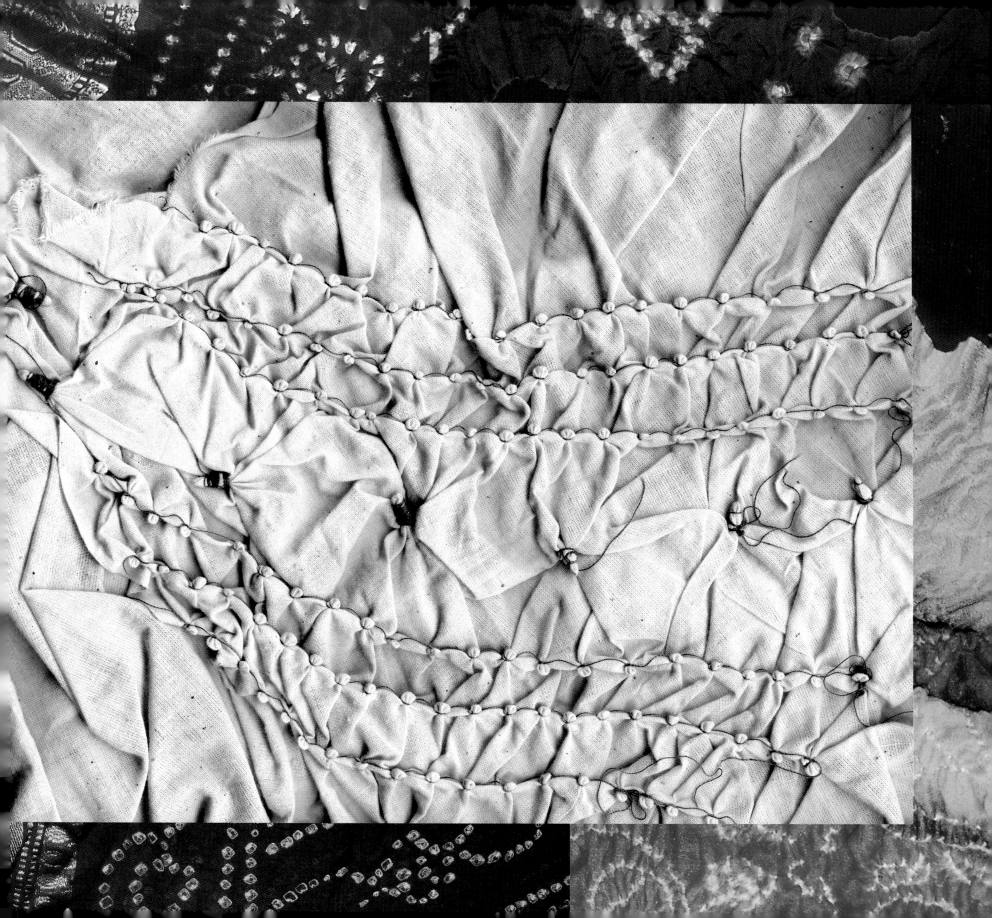

Mirrorwork embroidery *The Rabari nomads of Gujarat*

The dried marshes of the Rann of Kutch, in India's western state of Gujarat, are not an obvious tourist attraction, unless you are passionate about textiles and have fallen under the spell of the region's enchanting mirrorwork embroidery that shimmers in the sun.

The road out of Jaisalmer seems to go on for ever, lined with stunted acacia trees battered by the desert winds, but at last we reach Bhuj, in the Kutch heartland. From here we can branch out in all directions and visit the surrounding villages.

The monotony of the desert landscape is broken by the sight of a group of Rabari nomads and their herds approaching like figures out of a fairytale, a mirage from some long-lost Eden. Stretched out along the road are some ten camels laden with packsaddles and accompanied by their young. The sound of bells attached to the animals' hooves marks the caravan's progress. Each camel has a bed, or *charpoy*, tied to its hump, with a sleeping baby or, in some cases, a pregnant woman propped among the covers. Swinging from the uprights and clattering cheerfully are an assortment of milk cans and cooking pots, while the family's personal belongings are stuffed inside brown woollen bundles tied to the beast's flanks. Each camel is led by a woman whose full skirts sway as she walks, barefoot, holding the halter in one hand, gracefully erect under the pile of pots of water, milk and foodstuffs she carries on her head. The rear of the caravan is brought up by a camel harnessed to a cart carrying the old folk, the sick animals and the poultry. A herd of sheep and goats comes trotting and capering alongside, accompanied by dogs and shepherded by spindly children dressed in white with red turbans on their heads.

Each year, during the dry season, some five thousand Rabari families move about in caravans like this one, heading for fresh pasturelands.

In the village of Ludia, the Ahir women all come crowding around when they find out that I am interested in their embroideries. I am offered all manner of things: a baby's bonnet, a blouse yoke, a belt, a bag, a pouch to keep my dowry in. It is a delicate business because I want to be fair and avoid offending anyone. Banknotes exchange hands and I am very soon overwhelmed by a flurry of shimmering embroideries, mirrors, sequins, flying beads and rupees.

Above: The rectangular houses in Kutch are decorated with brightly coloured murals that resemble the local embroidery designs and are in total contrast to the hard, cracked earth of the region.

Opposite, left: Several layers of worn cotton are stitched together to form a soft, boldly coloured quilt edged with a piece of indented white appliqué.

Opposite, right: Hatti is a Meghwal woman from the village of Hodka. Putting down her embroidery, she explains:

'I embroider mirrors on the bodice, the belt, the back of the neck and the wrists. They create a barrier and protect the body from the evil spirits that are trying to find a way in.'

At Umra Kahana's house, in the village of Hodka. Umra, a Meghwal woman, makes quilted patchwork covers from second-hand cotton fabric. After we have finally struck a deal for one of her patchworks, we share a meal of goat stew.

Clockwise from top left:

The laced back of a Rabari blouse, a *kanchali*.

A small embroidered cushion called an *idani*, used for carrying pots on the head.

Bridegroom's bag, or *pothu*, designed to hold betel nuts to give to his guests.

Necklace on top of a black wool shawl decorated with a *bandhani* pattern in saffron yellow.

A dense embroidered design with mirror pieces.

Portrait of 'Mastani', a famous dancer, framed and displayed at the Aina Mahal, or Palace of Mirrors, at Bhuj.

Lakshmi and her son, in the village of Ludia. When a child is born, coconut oil is rubbed into its skin and its eyes and brows are highlighted with a thick line of kohl to chase away evil spirits.

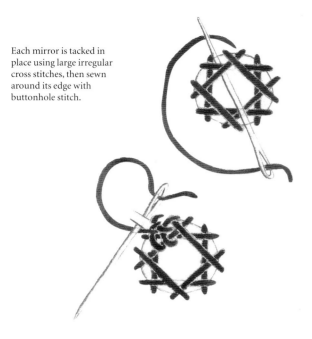

Each mirror is tacked in place using large irregular cross stitches, then sewn around its edge with buttonhole stitch.

This is a desert region, a vast area of dried-up salt marshes. Flashing in the sun's rays, the mirrors, or *shisha*, sewn onto the women's clothing, are a striking contrast to this cracked and arid wasteland, symbolizing light and life-giving fertility.

The Aina Mahal or Palace of Mirrors at Bhuj, which was damaged during the earthquake of January 2001, is a magnificent example of this cult of light. The local use of mirrorwork is connected with the deposits of mica, a sparkling silicate mineral, that were first discovered in the province of Sind, in Pakistan. Today's mirrors are produced in a former factory at Kapadvanj, in Gujarat, broken into small pieces and packaged at Limbdi, then sold in bazaars throughout the subcontinent.

Kutch: a desert full of people

The Rajputs are the landowners in this northwestern corner of India. The Rabari are a semi-nomadic pastoral people of Iranian descent who live in remote hamlets known as *dhanis*. The Maldari rear livestock for milk and meat. The Meghwal are leather workers. The Vedha carpenters carve furniture and wooden eating utensils. The light-eyed Jat are Muslims who make a living from farming and livestock. And the Ahir women make fabulous embroidery.

Both the men and the women dress extremely distinctively. The men wear white and a profusion of jewelry (although with no mirrors), including bracelets, rings, talismans and earrings, often attached to their upper ears, plus an impressive scarlet turban – the finishing touch to a look that is striking and elegant.

The women wear dark colours, including a skirt and veil both in black wool. 'Cotton won't grow here, but we have lots of wool,' a Rabari woman explains. The rough wool of the veil is dyed black, then embroidered with multicoloured patterns in buttonhole and cross stitch, and decorated with a tie-dye pinhead design in red or saffron yellow. The opening left by the veil reveals the *kanchali*, a short-sleeved blouse with an open laced back; the front is inlaid with mirrors, fixed in place with dense embroidery.

Rabari dress has inspired designers including Isabel Marant, and Rabari-style laced-up backless blouses and inlaid mirrorwork are recurrent themes in the fashion collections of the West.

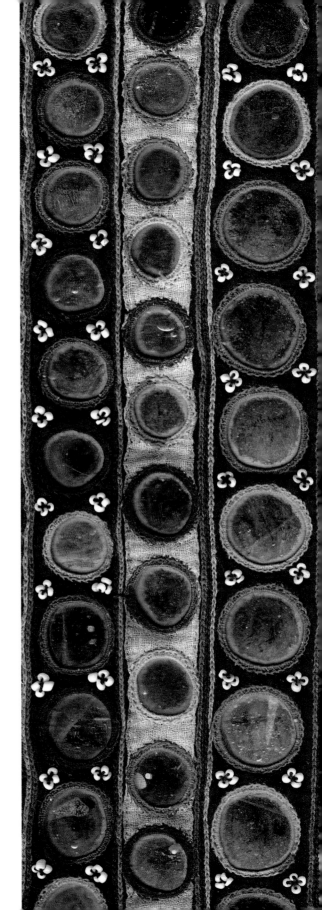

Right: Skirt belt with three rows of embroidered mirrors.

✳ Rabari women's clothing

The blouse, *kanchali* or *kapadu*, is very close-fitting and only has a front and sleeves, no fabric at the back, which is laced up. The embroidery at the front is shaped to fit the bust.

Small shopping bag, *kothali*, used by both men and women. The bag is decorated with mirrorwork embroidery and edged with a multicoloured cotton fringe.

Necklace.

Gathered skirt, *ghaghara*, worn by Mochi women and reserved for festivals. It is in black wool, tie-dyed with a red pinhead design. The gathers are sewn into an embroidered waistband and the bottom of the skirt is covered with embroidery and red cotton appliqué.

The veil or shawl, is known as a *ludi* by the Khachhi Rabari and a *phulakhiya ludaki* by the Vaghadia Rabari. It is made up of two lengths of wool joined together by a row of trailing stitch and decorated with a zigzag tie-dye pattern of orange and red dots. At each end, there is a broad panel of multicoloured embroidery in chain stitch, incorporating mirrors and sequins. Embroidered medallions are scattered over the shawl in accordance with strict design conventions, and each local subgroup can be identified by its style of weaving, embroidery motifs and fringe. Vaghadia Rabari women own at least three woollen shawls: a black *chotaru* with its blueish border for everyday use; a black *ludaki* with a saffron-yellow *bandhani* design for festivals, and an embroidered *phulakhiya ludaki*, reserved for weddings.

Opposite: An orange and black striped veil, *odhni*, in a satin weave combining a silk warp and a cotton weft, with panels of floral embroidery and mirrorwork at either end. This luxurious fabric is known as *mashru*, which translates as 'authorized'. In Islamic law, silk is not meant to come into direct contact with the body, so the cotton side of the veil is worn against the skin, and the shiny silk side on the exterior.

Elegance, Rajasthani style *Men's clothing and turbans*

In Mahatma Gandhi's struggle against imperialism, the spinning wheel and yarn became symbols of independence and a means of guaranteeing economic survival for Indian villages.

Sona Ram lives in a very isolated spot, but he has of course heard of Gandhi, who organized a boycott of British textiles in the 1920s, exhorting his fellow Indians to dispense with European clothes in favour of India's traditional costume, the loincloth of homespun cotton or khadi.

Opposite: Jewelry is not the sole preserve of women but represents a good investment for men too. Rajasthani men wear gold hoop or enamelled earrings and silver bracelets, along with amulets (*jantar*) and medals portraying images of the gods (*patri*) – both the latter as much for aesthetic as for religious reasons.

The *dhoti*, or loincloth

Sona Ram has always worn a *dhoti*, like his father and his grandfather before him. He has had no truck with stiff collars and jackets, the shackles of Gandhi's youth, or with the jodhpurs beloved of polo players. Sona Ram keeps things utterly simple: his *dhoti* doubles up as trousers, bag, scarf, towel and turban – and one day it will serve as his shroud.

The *dhoti*, or *lunghi*, is a long rectangle of cloth skilfully rolled to create the illusion of a pair of puffy trousers. When he is working, Sona Ram wears his above his knees like a pair of shorts, but as soon as he spots the camera, out of a sense of propriety or a wish for greater elegance, he tugs on the cloth and it falls down to meet his shoes, his *juti*. Depending on what he is doing, Sona Ram rolls up his *dhoti* on one thigh and lets it down on the other leg, so that he looks like a white wading bird standing on one foot.

The alternatives to the *dhoti* are wide-legged trousers known as *salwar*, and the *churidar*, trousers that cling to the calves but have a lot of fabric at the waist and are cut on the bias to allow for more movement. The cut of the *churidar* is influenced by Mughal styles, and they are worn at weddings accompanied by a long jacket with a stand-up collar, in either a plain or a richly embroidered fabric, reminiscent of the Maharajahs.

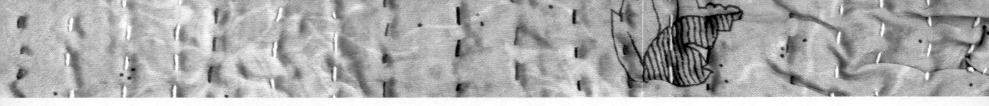

Rajasthani men's clothing

The turban, *pagri*, *pecha*, *safa* or *sela*, is a narrow band of fabric between 8 and 14 metres long. It can be white or coloured – red, saffron yellow and pink being regarded as the noblest colours – and may be plain or printed. Maharajah turbans were embellished with gorgeous jewels and an aigrette in the Mughal tradition. A Rajasthani will happily unroll his turban if he needs a rope to haul up a bucket of water for his camel or some means of securing and carrying a sick lamb.

The shawl or scarf.

The tunic, *angarakhi*, has a wide neck opening fastened with a round cloth button. It has a visible pocket at the front and another invisible one at the back, formed by a piece of decorative appliqué which also serves the purpose of reinforcing the garment.

The undershirt, *baniyan*, *bandhi* or *ureb baniyan*, is bias cut for ease of movement and has a vertical pocket trimmed with piping.

A pair of trousers, *churidar*, can be worn in place of the *dhoti*.

The *dhoti*, an unhemmed rectangle generally measuring 1.2 by 4 metres.

Opposite, above: A Dhebaria Rabari man's smock, known as a *kediyun*. It is made of delicately embroidered cotton, enhanced with sequins. The cut dates back to the 15th century and is thought to be Mughal. The jacket is worn with trousers, *chorani*, that are generously cut at the top and more clinging on the legs. The effect is very elegant, combining fullness at the waist, closely fitting arms, legs and torso, and soft petal-like skirts on the jacket.

The jacket is made up of three parts:

1. a short upper section cut from a single piece of double thickness cloth that forms the back and front

2. an embroidered double collar

3. a wide pleated panel forming the body of the jacket.

The pleats are gathered at the top and the jacket has white tie fastenings with coloured cotton ends.

Opposite, below: The owner's name is embroidered on the front in Gujarati.

The Rajasthani tunic, the *angarakhi*

The *achakan*, or *angarakhi*, is a white cotton tunic with a deep front opening and narrow sleeves, and is commonly used by Rajasthani men for everyday wear: it is the sort of garment you can see in Mughal miniatures. It is worn next to the skin, and exposes a hint of chest in the gap at the front. Sona Ram picks and chooses between an *angarakhi*, a Western shirt and a sleeveless top, known as a *bandhi*. 'The *angarakhi* and the *bandhi* are ingenious garments, with lots of hidden pockets where I keep a few rupees and my packet of cigarettes,' he says. 'If I need a bag, I tie my scarf into one.' The only accessory these men carry is a cotton scarf, a beige woollen shawl thrown over one shoulder, or a black and white checked blanket for warmth at night in the Thar Desert.

No drab grey suits or blue jeans here: the men wear gleaming white – an attire which is very much to their credit, given the rigours of daily life and the absence of running water in the majority of homes. Like many Indians living in rural areas, Sona Ram tells us that he goes at dawn each morning to the *ghats*, the steps leading down to the lake, where he practises his ritual ablutions, washing both himself and his clothes.

Instead of the *dhoti*, Muslim Indians wear a white cotton outfit called a *salwar kameez* or *kurta pyjama* – a pair of wide-legged trousers and a long shirt with or without a collar. Over the top, they wear a gilet or waistcoat.

Mange Lal puts his hands together in greeting (the *namaste*). At 74, he still looks extremely elegant.

Above: In the village of Javasia, near Pipar, Sona Ram is hanging out his washing. The 66-year-old is slight and wiry. with a neatly clipped moustache. He wears his hair cropped very short – with the exception of a single strand, left long for religious reasons.

Right: Made of layers of leather sewn together, a basic shoe sole looks fairly crude – little different from a clog. But once the leather is dyed, and the curved toe is in place, and once the upper has been embroidered in chain stitch with silk, wool or cotton threads – by the hands of female embroiderers – and embellished with pompoms, sequins and gold thread, a simple shoe is transformed into a work of art.

Overleaf: Turbans of all colours.

Traditional turbans

The only hint of colour in a Rajasthani man's outfit is his turban, called a *pagri, paag* or *safa*. Turbans can be white, as a sign of mourning or to indicate that the wearer is a strict vegetarian, but for the most part they are coloured. Rabari men wear a heavily coiled turban in a really strong red. Saffron yellow and fuchsia pink are common elsewhere, while in Udaipur the turban is tie-dyed in a variety of colours. Turbans are worn in different ways depending on region and caste: a turban not only protects the wearer from the desert winds and the sun; it is also a badge of identity, revealing the ethnic group to which he belongs. Muslim men may either wear a turban or a small white cap.

The interchange between Mughal and Hindu traditions has resulted in a great cultural richness in terms of architecture, music and dress, in which both Hindu and Muslim groups borrow from the other. In northern India, increasing numbers of young Hindu women – particularly students – choose to wear the *salwar kameez* in preference to the sari for ease of movement. And whereas high-ranking Rajputs used to employ people, known

as *pagriband*, to wind their turbans for them, the young men of today tend to prefer a cricket cap. We may perhaps be witnessing the last generation of turbaned heads, and perhaps of moustaches too, since these two often go together.

In rural areas, men take enormous care of their moustaches, which may be black, grey or white, or dyed with henna; and accompanied by a beard or sideburns, clipped in a military style, or twirled or slicked using the fingers. Itinerant barbers work in the open air and the immediate future still looks rosy for them.

Juti

These finely made shoes are worn by both men and women and sewn from goat's or sheep's hide by members of the shoemakers' caste. Despite the invasion of trainers and plastic flip-flops, *juti* are still bravely holding their own, and every village in Rajasthan has a workshop where they are made to measure – just like the most luxurious footwear in the West.

Signs of belonging *Jewelry and henna*

The legend of Mira Bai has fuelled the dreams of young Indian girls for centuries. Mira Bai was a young princess and poet in the 16th century, daughter of a nobleman from Marwa. She married into a princely family from Udaipur but was widowed at a very young age, and took advantage of her new-found freedom to devote her life to Krishna, whom she had worshipped since childhood. She left the court to become a wandering minstrel and went to live in Brindaban, Krishna's native village. The story goes that she was dancing one day to the sound of a flute in front of a portrait of the god, when Krishna himself appeared and whisked her away…

Jewelry

All Indian women wear jewelry, regardless of their level of wealth, decking themselves from head to toe – with earrings, nose studs, forehead pendants, necklaces, belts, bracelets, rings, hand ornaments, anklets, toe rings and more. Every bit of exposed skin is a potential display case. The poorest peasant woman can be decorated like a princess, her every movement accompanied by clinking bracelets and tinkling ankle bells. The only women who are barred from wearing jewelry are widows. Jewelry, like clothing, serves to identify caste and social status, and indicates whether or not a woman is married, but it also represents her dowry and her sole fortune, her fall-back and protection against hard times, since these Indian women are not traditionally entitled to own land.

Body ornaments are endowed with curative, protective and talismanic powers. The pressure exerted by the weight of an earring, for example, impacts directly on one of the body's internal organs, and anklets with bells attached are thought to frighten off snakes. Newborn babies are given a talisman to wear round their neck and silver anklets as soon as they start to walk.

Rajasthan is a region rich in mineral deposits and precious stones. It has always been famous for its jewelry, and Jaipur's lapidaries are regarded as masters of the art of cutting and setting gemstones in the *kundankari* tradition using hammered gold wire.

Ulfat is a young Muslim girl from Borunda, with striking green eyes. She has put on all her finery to celebrate the end of Ramadan – necklace, earrings and forehead pendant, held in place with a little pink clip – and resembles like a princess from *The Thousand and One Nights*. She has also decorated her hands with *mehndi* specially for the occasion.

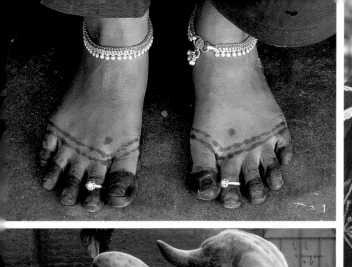

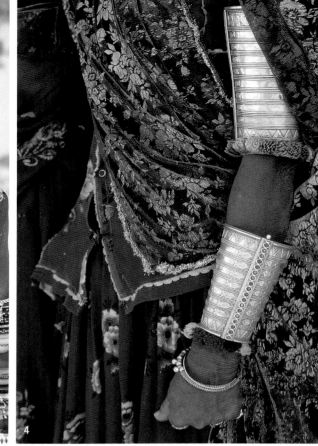

1. Sherbano's feet, decorated with henna and with anklets and toe rings.

2. A cow tattooed with henna for the festival of Holi. The cow belongs to members of the Garasia tribe, near Udaipur.

3. Young woman wearing an array of gold and silver jewelry, including a gold nose ring (*nath*), and clothes made from brightly coloured synthetic material.

4. 'These bracelets are all I have,' says Sita. 'If trouble should come, I'll sell one. I have a beautiful pair of earrings too. They're buried in the earth, under the floor of my house, so nobody can take them.'

5. Surya is wearing a forehead ornament and an adhesive *tilak*.

6. A Rabari woman working for a stonemason – wearing all her jewelry.

7. The henna patterns on a mother and daughter's hands look like block-printed designs on fabric.

Silver was associated with the moon in former times and is more commonly worn in rural areas, while wealthy city dwellers tend to prefer gold inlaid with pearls and precious stones, or enamelled in the Mughal tradition. Every large village has its jewellers' caste, the *sonar*, who are responsible for making wedding jewelry and ornaments. Bracelets made from ivory, plastic, horn, ceramic or silver are popular with Rajasthani women, who wear them all the way up their arms. Necklaces are often decorated with braided ties and coloured tassels. And talismans are widely worn among Rabari men, hung around the neck on a piece of cord with a red tassel hanging down the back. A piece of cotton yarn tied around the wrist is also commonly worn by both men and women as a protective symbol.

Mehndi or henna

Rajasthani women from both Hindu and Muslim backgrounds decorate their hands and feet with henna, which is not only regarded as attractive but also thought to ward off bad luck. The red colour of the *mehndi* is associated with Gangaur – the festival of spring held in honour of the goddess Parvati – and with good fortune and success in love. The young girls in Sherbano's house, in Jodhpur, celebrate the end of Ramadan by mixing powdered henna leaves and oil and filling plastic cones with the paste, which they then use to draw flowers and swirling patterns on their feet and on both sides of their hands. The paste dries to a powder and falls off, revealing the patterns on the skin, and the colour can be freshened by massaging in a few drops of oil. 'It's strict tradition whenever anyone gets married. The bride's henna decorations guarantee a happy union: the rite is a natural part of the ceremony,' explains Sherbano, while she sews and waits for the *mehndi* that has been freshly applied to her feet to dry.

The *tilak* or *bindi*: the dot on the forehead

The *tilak* is intriguing. It is a dot painted on the forehead, between the eyebrows, to represent the third eye – the eye that sees the truth that lies beyond appearances. The dot is painted afresh each day. After her morning purification, my friend Prabah blackens her right middle finger on the wick of the sesame oil lamp burning on the household altar. '*Til* means "sesame", which is why we call the dot *tilak*, *tilaka* or *tika*,' she explains to me. 'Some families prefer to use a bright red paste, *sindoor* or *kumkum*, instead of soot. It is applied as a dot or in a line along the hair parting.' *Sadhu*, or holy men, also make marks on their forehead: the followers of Shiva draw three horizontal lines with sandalwood paste or ash, and the followers of Vishnu wear a vertical white line inside a red V.

Today, the *tilak* is becoming more of a fashion statement and in the markets you can buy self-adhesive discs in various shapes – a halfway house between the traditional dot and the forehead ornament known as a *chutti*. Prabah lets me into some of her other beauty secrets: 'For my nails, I use the sap of the maldroni plant. It's bright red. I rub coconut oil into my hair to make it shine, and I put *kajal*, powdered antimony, round my eyes. Ever since they were born, I have painted kohl on my sons' eyebrows and eyelids: it's symbolic and it also works as a disinfectant.'

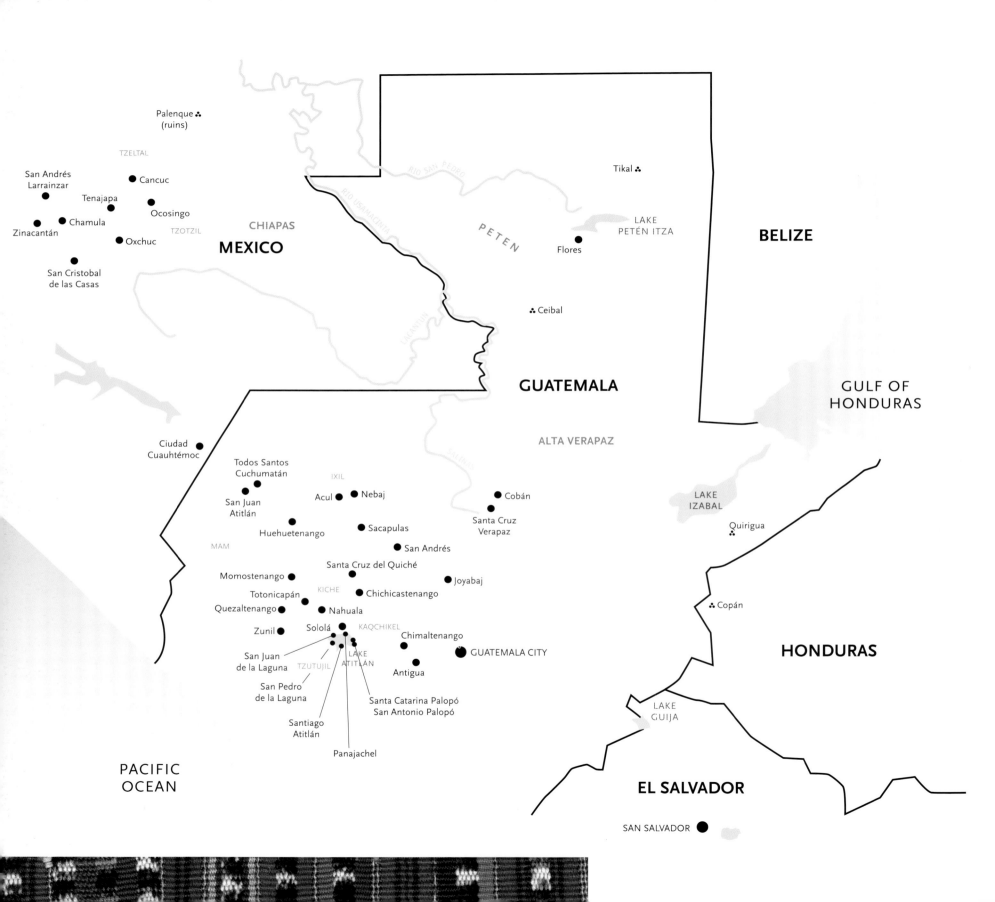

Palenque ☘
(ruins)

TZELTAL

San Andrés
Larrainzar ●
● Cancuc
Tenajapa ●
Chamula ● Ocosingo ●
Zinacantán ●
● Oxchuc
TZOTZIL

CHIAPAS

MEXICO

San Cristobal
de las Casas ●

RIO USAMACINTA

RIO SAN PEDRO

Tikal ☘

PETEN

LAKE
PETÉN ITZA

BELIZE

Flores ●

☘ Ceibal

GUATEMALA

GULF OF
HONDURAS

ALTA VERAPAZ

Ciudad ●
Cuauhtémoc

Todos Santos
Cuchumatán ●
IXIL
Acul ● ● Nebaj
● Cobán
San Juan
Atitlán ●
Huehuetenango ● ● Sacapulas
Santa Cruz
Verapaz

LAKE
IZABAL

Quirigua ☘

MAM
● San Andrés
Santa Cruz del Quiché ●
Momostenango ● ● Joyabaj
Totonicapán ● KICHE ● Chichicastenango
Quezaltenango ● ● Nahuala
Zunil ● Sololá KAQCHIKEL
San Juan ● ● Chimaltenango
de la Laguna TZUTUJIL LAKE
ATITLÁN ● GUATEMALA CITY
San Pedro ● Antigua
de la Laguna
Santa Catarina Palopó
San Antonio Palopó
Santiago
Atitlán
Panajachel

Copán ☘

HONDURAS

LAKE
GUIJA

PACIFIC
OCEAN

EL SALVADOR

SAN SALVADOR ●

Mexico and Guatemala
A Mayan mosaic

Guatemala and the Mexican state of Chiapas may be on opposite sides of the border, but they share a common identity that goes back to the pre-Columbian world and the culture of the ancient Mayans, whose relics remain scattered from Mexico to Honduras.

Another facet of this identity is the religious syncretism of the region, in which Christianity has been integrated into an existing belief system that encompasses Mayan cosmology, shamanic practices and the legends contained in the sacred book, the *Popol Vuh*. The Mayan language is divided up into a mosaic of dialects that continue to be spoken in preference to Spanish, and distinctive traditional costumes are still worn by the various peoples of the region – de facto majorities that are nevertheless minorities in terms of power.

This is a world where crossing the *río*, skirting the foot of the volcano, or negotiating a path through the *selva* is like stepping into a rainbow. The world of the sacred quetzal, the turkey and the coyote. A world where the blue of indigo mingles with the red of cochineal, the pink of bougainvilleas and the mauve of morning glory.

Here, a woman weaves the way she cooks, making not only everything she needs herself – her blouse (*huipil*), skirt (*corte* or *falda*), shawl (*perraje* or *tzute*), belts and hair bands, but also clothes for her children and – if he has not adopted a Western style of dress – her husband too.

Using a traditional backstrap loom (*telar de cintura*), attached to a tree or the post of a house, and following the conventions of their respective villages, Mayan women weave simple lengths of cloth, sometimes in a brocade style and embellished with stripes, flowers, a snake, or a motif evoking thunder – the story of their Mayan identity in images.

The thread of identity

Indigo *In the depths of the dye baths*

The man with blue hands is Mexican. He lives in a quiet suburb of San Cristobal de las Casas, a **barrio** *or district of Tlaxcala, away from the tourists, the roar of traffic and the brash shopkeepers. He has set up his dye shed in a corner of his backyard, under the mango, lemon and peach trees.*

Previous pages, left: A little girl from Zinacantán, Chiapas, wearing an indigo skirt embroidered with large purple flowers and turquoise leaves. The women of her village grow flowers to sell and their embroidery continues the floral theme.

Previous pages, right: View of a cemetery on the road to Tenejapa, Chiapas.

Opposite: Sandra has just come back from school and is helping her father. She keeps an eye on the vats, but is not involved in the actual dyeing. She hangs the skeins out to dry on the terrace and winds the bobbins and takes them to the weavers working in Felipe's workshop at the bottom of the garden.

Felipe is one of the last hand-dyers in San Cristobal, Chiapas. He is reserved and soft-spoken. He talks about his work with pride, though there is a hint of bitterness when he describes the hard years he served as an apprentice. When asked if he intends to pass on his skills to his children, he answers: 'No, I don't think so. Antonio [his 12-year-old son] is good at maths. I'm saving up to buy him a computer because at the moment he has to do his homework in a cybercafé.'

Felipe can barely read or write, but he is extremely knowledgeable about dyeing and weaving. Indigo (*Indigofera suffruticosa*) grows in El Salvador, from where it used to be exported to Mexico and Guatemala, while cotton was formerly grown in plantations on Mexico and Guatemala's Pacific coast. 'Today, I go to Puebla to buy American cotton and powdered anil or indigo, *el azul alemán*, imported from Germany.' Felipe is preparing his vat of anil and tastes the mixture to test its acidity. For a good strong blue, he says, '*Hay que quemar en la boca* – It's got to burn.'

Felipe holding a piece of indigo. His hands are always stained blue.

'At the age of 8, I had to leave my native village and come and work as an apprentice for a dyer in San Cristobal.'

As a fixative, he dissolves soda in water that has first been filtered through ash – the same recipe I have found people using on the Chinese border and in Benin. The superstitions seem to be universal too: 'Pregnant women are supposed to keep away from the vat,' Felipe says, 'or the dye will turn.' But he also gives a rational explanation: 'The fermentation process gives off gases that are harmful to the unborn baby.' It is certainly true that the vats give off a peculiar smell – the distinctive scent of indigo. The dye bath is a greenish colour, and with each immersion, the blue of the yarn intensifies. Fashions vary from village to village, and Felipe soaks his yarn several times to get the shade of blue required by individual customers. In a workshop at the bottom of the garden, two men are weaving on pedal-operated looms. They weave rolls of indigo cloth measuring 50 *baras* each (about 40 metres by 80 centimetres), producing some 18 metres of cloth a day. The cloth is sold in rolls in the markets and is used to sew *cortes*, *morgas* and *faldas*, skirts that require between 3 and 4 metres of fabric.

Above: The yarn has been hung to dry on the terrace during a sunny spell, in between two tropical downpours. 'In San Cristobal de las Casas, it rains a great deal in the summer, which slows things down for me.' Felipe says. 'On rainy days, I don't do any dyeing and the cotton doesn't dry. The dampness makes the weaving irregular. The selvedge crinkles up. And the weavers stop coming in.'

Right, above and centre: Indigo plants and indigo powder.

Right, below: The art of natural dyemaking is no mystery to the women of the San Juan Chamula cooperative.

Opposite: The cycle of Felipe's working life is summed up by the objects on this blue chair. He buys skeins of white cotton from a wholesaler in Puebla, dyes the cotton and weaves it into cloth from which skirts will eventually be made. Rolls of indigo cotton like this one are sold in the markets near Ocosingo, where Felipe comes from.

The colours of Chiapas

Visiting the community of Bautista Chico, on the edge of San Juan Chamula, is like opening a box of paints. The women of the cooperative know all about natural dyes and let us into a few secrets.

Red and lilac are obtained from the *palo de campecho*, a yellow-flowered tree that grows in the mangrove swamps of southeast Mexico. The branches and the heartwood yield a beautiful red colour.

Reddish brown is obtained from the *palo de brasil*, a tree that grows in Guerrero, Jalisco and Michoacán.

Brown is extracted from walnut shells.

Yellow comes from a parasitical plant, *xacatlaxcali* or *barba de león*, which is found all over the hedgerows.

Blue is produced by fermenting *muitle* leaves.

Indigo is produced by fermenting the leaves of the indigo plant. It is known locally as *sacatinta* and *jiquilite*.

Red is obtained from the cochineal insect or *grana*, which lives as a parasite on a common cactus called the nopal. The females are collected when they are full of eggs, dried and crushed in a mortar, and the powder obtained by this process is mixed with water and lemon juice (which serves as a mordant) and heated gently. This traditional dye technique dates back to before 500 BC.

Purple is made from the secretions of a shellfish, *Purpura patula*, which is harvested on the shores of Guerrero and Oaxaca: it takes between 90 and 150 shells to produce 200 grams of dye. This technique dates back to the pre-Columbian era.

Bright green is obtained from the *palo de mula* or *palo amarillo*, a tree growing in the Peten region of Guatemala.

Black, *lodo*, is obtained from a mixture of sediments rich in metallic oxides collected from river beds and kept in vats.

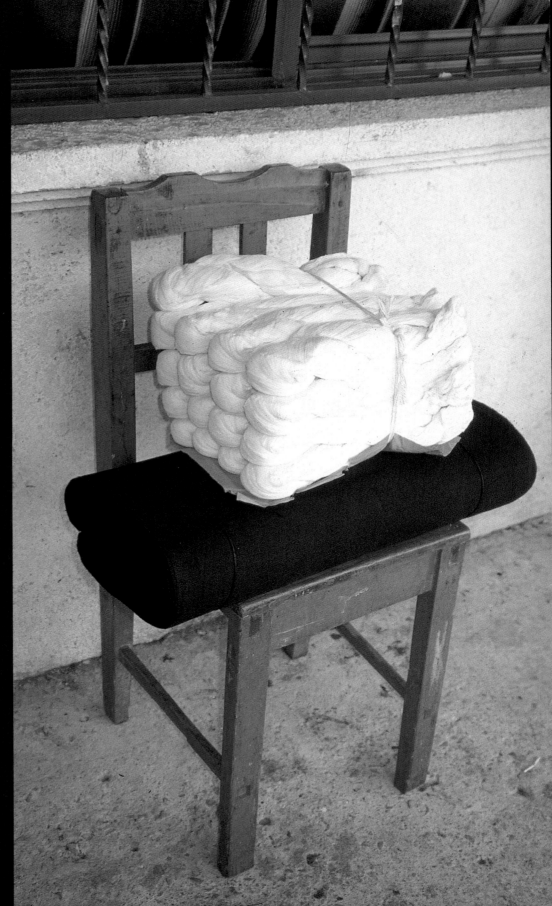

The Mayan skirt *Variations on a theme*

Mayan women from Guatemala and Chiapas love skirts: they never wear trousers, no matter what age they are and no matter what job they are doing. A woman's skirt is her passport to elegance and the skirt is like a leitmotif linking one village to the next in endless minor variations. Chiapas, generally, has a preference for indigo, but some villages opt instead for a striped or brocaded look.

The Mayan skirt (*morga*) is a simple tube made up of a single panel or several panels fixed together with a band of embroidery known as a *randa*. The skirt can be between 2 and 5 metres wide and the superfluous material is gathered into one or two pleats held in place by a woven belt. The *randa* is embroidered using mercerized cotton or silk thread and the motifs vary between villages, so that the wearer's origins can be identified at a glance.

A mother and child in San Andrés Larrainzar, Chiapas.

Below: a multicoloured *randa*, used to disguise a skirt seam.

Opposite, from top to bottom and left to right:

Women from Zunil, Guatemala, wearing two different styles of *cortes*. The striped skirt is in the Chichicastelnango style; the other is a brocade skirt in the contemporary Zunil style.

Close-up of the patterns on a Zunil skirt.

Skirt from Sololá, Guatemala, with *jaspeado* stripes.

San Andrés Larrainzar, Chiapas. Alexandra's skirt is decorated with a *randa* of multicoloured embroidery in trailing stitch. Her broad red belt is fastened with two braided ties.

In Tenejapa, Chiapas, the *randa* is made up of embroidered circular motifs.

Sketch showing how a skirt is folded.

In Ococingo, Chiapas, multicoloured synthetic braid is sewn onto a length of indigo cloth in place of woven stripes.

The secrets of *jaspe*

The jaspe *technique produces beautiful woven effects reminiscent of the gemstone jasper, a microcrystalline form of quartz found in shades of red, green, brown and black and marked with delicate bands.*

What makes *jaspe* so beautiful is the fact that no two stripes are quite the same. The patterning is controlled but irregular, a subtle shimmering of colours, with light merging into shadow and shadow merging into light.

Jaspeado cloth is like a woven painting, leaving space for the imagination. It might recall the sea, or rippled sand, a mythical creature, a lyre, a flower, a river, a plume of feathers, a whole array of intentional and unintentional patterns. *Jaspe* is the American Indian name, derived from Spanish, for the ikat technique, an international language of tied and dyed threads that is practised in places from Sambalpur to Totonicapán, from Chiang Rai to Dassa, from Kuala Lumpur to Ahmedabad, and from Bukhara to the Ryukyu Islands.

American Indian women are fond of shawls and skirts in *jaspeado* cloth, and the demand for these products is keeping the technique alive among Guatemalan dyers and weavers.

Guatemalan cloth uses all three types of ikat: warp ikat (*jaspe de urdimbre*), in which the *jaspeado* threads are mounted on the warp parallel to the selvedge (for *tzutes* or shawls); weft ikat (*jaspe de trama*), in which the *jaspeado* threads are perpendicular to the selvedge (for *cortes* or skirts); and compound ikat, in which two sets of *jaspeado* threads intersect to form patterns.

Above, top: Skeins of tied yarn.

Above, bottom: Doña Antonia's fabric store in Zunil.

Opposite, top left: The church in Zunil.

Opposite, right: Marta unravelling tied yarn to help her mother in her shop. Men, women and children all wear blouses with *jaspeado* designs, and the market place at Sololá is a kaleidoscope of colours.

The Santa Ana de Zunil cooperative

This women's weaving cooperative is located just below the charming white church in Zunil, a Kaqchikel village perched between volcanoes and maize plantations at an altitude of 2,000 metres.

Today is Monday, market day, and women are coming and going with bundles of weaving under their arms. The village is buzzing. At the cooperative, Doña Antonia greets us warmly. This is a lively place, with a shop selling *huipiles*, *cortes* and *tzutes*, each garment bearing a label with the name of its maker. In the next room is a drapery where the weavers can buy yarn, spools, reeds for looms, needles, scissors and skeins of *jaspeado* thread at wholesale prices.

Women who want to sell *jaspeado* yarn to local weavers can learn the technique by attending workshops run by experts invited by the cooperative and held in the assembly room. The *jaspe* used by the designer John Galliano for one of his collections was woven by members of the very dynamic Zunil cooperative.

Dolores Zinay Chiviliu lives in Santiago Atitlán. She has just turned eighteen, but is already an expert at tying yarn.

Opposite: Weavers in the garden of a house in Santiago Atitlán wearing the flowered *huipil* and *Jaspeado* skirts for which Santiago is famous. The red yarn they are holding is a symbol of solidarity.

Left: *Jaspeado* cloth from San Juan de la Laguna, valued by collectors and textile designers for its soft, thick cotton and the naturalness and subtlety of its colours.

Santiago Atitlán *jaspeado*

As we go from house to house in Santiago Atitlán – nestling beside Atitlán Lake – we are met with the same scene: behind every closed door, women with incredibly nimble fingers are busy tying cotton threads.

They are producing weft *jaspe*, tying selected threads stretched between the uprights of a frame. The tied yarn will go to a weaver and be turned into the finely woven skirts (*cortes*) for which the village is famous.

Salcaja and Totonicapán *jaspeado*

Salcaja and the neighbouring towns of Totonicapán and Quezaltenango together form Guatemala's largest manufacturing centre, the *pueblo del jaspe*, specializing in weft *jaspe*. The town produces both woven cloth and skeins of tied yarn which are sold to the weavers of the surrounding villages. The cotton is ginned, spun and dyed industrially, but the *jaspeado* yarn is tied and dyed by hand, and in fine weather Salcaja is festooned with hundreds of skeins of drying yarn.

San Juan de la Laguna *jaspeado*

The shawls (*rebozos*) from San Juan and the neighbouring villages, around Atitlán Lake, are woven in a brown and beige cotton known as *cuyuscate* or *ixcaco*, which is locally grown and hand-spun. Incorporated into the coffee-and-cream-coloured striped weave are blue *jaspe* stripes, made from natural cotton that has been tied and soaked in indigo. Due to the rarity of the raw material, this is an expensive fabric, reserved for special occasions.

Left: A draper unravelli[ng] *jaspeado* yarn at Sololá market. Her blouse and skirt are a perfect examp[le] of garments that rely on this technique.

Opposite: At Don Bernardo's workshop n[ear] Salcaja, his little girls – Carmen Marixela and Sandra Michaela – wear *jaspeado* blouses and ski[rts] as they sneak between th[e] looms and spinning whe[els] and play among the bobbins and piles of clot[h.]

Opposite: top left and bottom right: Samples of *jaspeado* cloth in the Totonicapán style.

Shawls, bundles and bags *Surviving traditions*

The shawl, *rebozo* or *tzute*

Folded in half lengthwise and thrown over the shoulder, the *rebozo* is an elegant shawl. Folded over and worn flat on the head, it shades the face or serves as a support for a basket. It can be tied and worn as a cape in cold weather – or as a veil, in church, to cover the hair. It can be filled with shopping, tied into a bundle and plumped on top of the head – as a *tzute* – or used to carry flowers to church or wood for fuel.

When used as a baby-carrier, it is known as a *cargador*. On the arm of a saint's statue, it becomes an offering. In a procession, it can be used to carry candles or ritual objects so as not to touch them directly with the hands, and takes on a ceremonial meaning.

A crucial item of women's dress, both in Mexico and Guatemala, the *rebozo*, or *perraje*, as it is known in the Mayan language, is a long shawl made from one or two panels of material which lends itself to multiple uses. It is woven on a backstrap loom in cotton or wool, or sometimes a silk and cotton or cotton and rayon mix, and finished with large tassels or a fringe.

A trip to the market will involve taking several shawls, and one of them will almost certainly be used to carry the shopping. Such colourful bulging bundles, stuffed with mysterious objects, can be seen scattered along the side of a street, often grouped in twos and threes, lined up patiently along a wall, forming a queue for a taxi or waiting to be hoisted on to the roof of a brightly coloured bus.

There is a something rather anthropomorphic about the *tzute*: its roundness gives a sense of generosity and plenitude, and the four firmly tied ends suggest a certain determination.

The *bolse, guangocha, morral* or *matate* – bags for men

Since there are no pockets in the traditional Mayan costume, a bag is also an indispensable part of a man's outfit. It is worn over the shoulder and goes with him everywhere – to town, to the fields, and travelling from place to place. He will put his smoking supplies in it, his machete and a few tortillas or *tamalitos* for lunch. Crocheted bags are made using cotton, wool or a natural fibre called *pita*, from the agave plant, or *maguey*. Crochet is a technique that was introduced by the Spanish and it has been adopted in numerous villages such as Todos Santos Cuchumátan and Sololá in Guatemala, where it is practised by the men. Brocaded or embroidered bags, on the other hand, are woven on a backstrap loom and are the work of the women.

When the rest of a traditional costume is abandoned, the bag remains as sole survivor, sole evidence of ancient customs. Fragile evidence, at that: given the number of market stalls selling Chinese-made backpacks, one can only suspect that its days are numbered, although the tourist trade is keeping the craft alive for the moment.

Above, top: Carmen Victoria goes shopping in the market at Zunil. She has a folded *rebozo* on her head and another one thrown over her shoulder.

Above, bottom: Bundles of shopping waiting to be hoisted on to the roof of a bus for the journey home. A smaller version of the *tzute* is used for keeping tortillas warm.

Opposite: Plastic baskets like these ones are woven in a small factory in Totonicapán. They are both practical and attractive, the coloured trims reminiscent of textile designs.

Wool from the high plateaux

Trapped in a thick mist, the black and white sheep (borregos) are dotted about on the green slopes of the mountains around San Cristobal de las Casas, Chiapas, and the grasslands of Guatemala's high plateaux.

It was only with the arrival of the conquistadors and the Catholic missionaries that sheep – formerly unknown in these regions in the time of the Mayans – were introduced to Central America.

In the market at San Juan Chamula, raw wool is displayed and sold loose, by weight. Before it is used, it will be washed, carded and combed between the bristles of two iron brushes, then spun by hand or using a spinning wheel. Rolled into a ball, it will be handwoven, and sometimes felted, to give some protection from the cold to communities living at an altitude in excess of 2,000 metres.

The women of San Juan use raw wool like this to make not only ponchos for their husbands, but also skirts for themselves, from circles of felted wool that are folded over at the waist for warmth, considerably thickening their waistline. While this traditional skirt, happily, continues to survive changing fashions, the woollen shawl, or *rebozo de lana*, is gradually being replaced by dreary acrylic cardigans that can be bought in the markets.

In Guatemala, wool is used for men's clothing too, including the coats (*capixay*) produced at San Juan Atitlán and the striped jackets of the Sololá region. It is also used to make a bag (*morral*) crocheted by the men. Momostenango is a large manufacturing centre where bedcovers (*serapes*) and carpets are woven, and also the *ponchitos*, or loincloths, worn by the men of Sololá, Nahuala and San Antonio Palopó. Upstream from the town, the wool is washed in the river, then softened in sulphur-rich water and later combed with a *quich*, a roller made from dried plants.

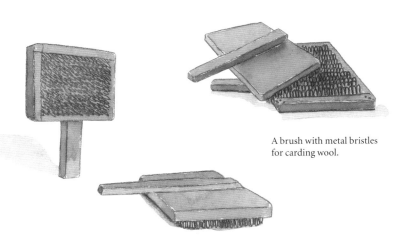

A brush with metal bristles for carding wool.

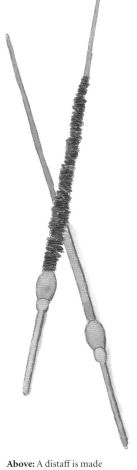

Above: A distaff is made of a ball of baked clay with a stick running through it.

Opposite: Mariano Batista Jimenez Coyasso wearing a white poncho – *erkoil* in Tzotzil. Ponchos like this one are worn by the men of the San Juan Chamula community in Chiapas.

Rosa Batista de la Cruz keeps an eye on her sheep while carding and spinning wool.

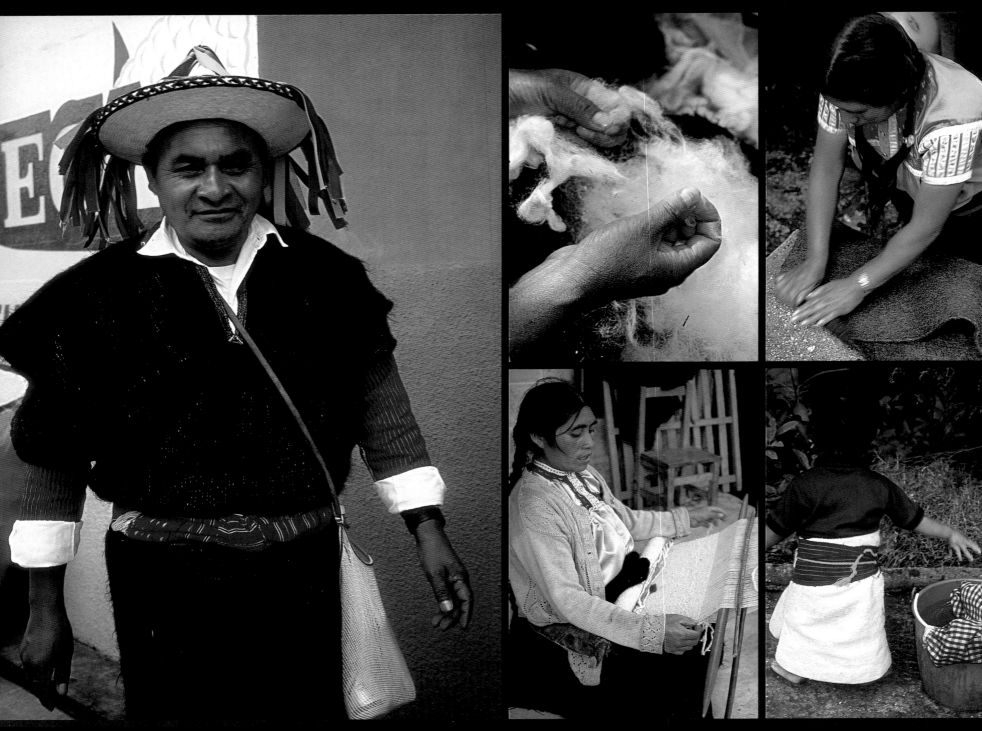

like dough, she explains: *'I use cold water to make felt. This grey wool is going to be a skirt, and I'm matting the fibres together by pressing down and beating it with my hands. Felting stops the wind and rain getting in. Black wool is more expensive than grey or white wool.'*

Above: For a festival today, Manuel Santiz Gomez wears the costume of the San Andrés Larrainzar *confradias* of Chiapas. His tunic is made of combed black wool.

Far right, below: This little girl is wrapped against the cold in a woollen skirt with

Above, centre: We walk through the maize fields to get to the home of Pascualita, who runs the Chamula women's association. While her mother, Juana, carries on with her weaving, Pascualita explains: *'Good-quality wool is combed to give a finer weave and a fluffy look. Two widths are used side by side to make the men's white or black ponchos.'*

Above: Maria Lopez Lopez from Chamula, Chiapas, wears a woollen tunic (*huipil*) and shawl (*rebozo*). The top is made of three widths of woollen cloth stitched edge to edge with green cotton. The wool is a natural brown colour, decorated with stripes of blue cotton threaded with white.

 Elegance for everyone

Flowers and stripes *The poetry of the* huipil

A rectangle of cotton, with an opening for the head: what could be simpler? But once the women have finished with it, this striped and embroidered rectangle of cotton is not just a practical piece of clothing but a work of art. Giant peonies and immaculate calla lilies, the mauve trumpets of the morning glory and the blood-red blooms of the pomegranate unfold their petals against a frame of vibrant stripes, entwined with leafy stems. Here, we see the Mayan cosmic serpent rearing its plumed head, there a roaming coyote. The quetzal perches in the topmost branches of the ceiba, *the sacred kapok tree, while among the tobacco plants, two hummingbirds flutter and dive: the* huipil *is a living book in whose pages the Mayan world and its symbols are unfurled.*

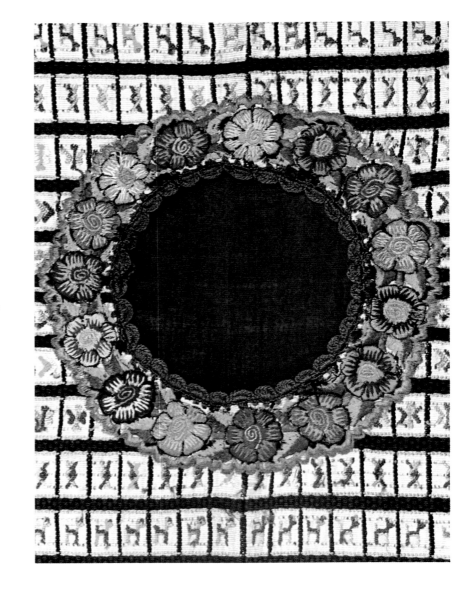

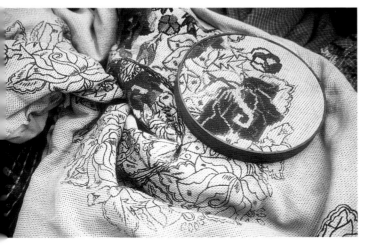

Above: The women like to chat as they work: '*Elvira is good at embroidery, but she's not from round here. This pattern is from the next village.*'

Maria advises: '*A huipil needs to be washed in cold water, preferably in a mountain stream. You have to dry it flat on the grass so it doesn't lose its shape, and also inside out to protect the colours.*'

Opposite: The collar of a Santiago Atitlán *huipil*, embroidered with flowers and finished with a crocheted purple trim. The *huipil* consists of two panels of striped white cotton decorated with a small woven pattern.

The cotton that grows along Mexico and Guatemala's tropical coastline produces a dense and supple cloth that is easy to weave, dye and embroider and can tolerate extensive washing in the river or the washtub.

This cotton is the very simple backcloth for the traditional Mayan blouse, the *huipil*, which is composed of one or two or sometimes three panels, or widths, woven on a backstrap loom. The join between the woven rectangles can be invisible – disguised by the patterning of the cloth – or it can become a piece of decorative embroidery in its own right, known as a *randa*.

The cloth is folded in half and a neck opening is made, which can either be a simple slit or a square, round or triangular cut-out hole. The side seams end at the armpit to form the armhole. The decoration on the *huipil* is focused around the neck, shoulders and armholes, and as well as looking good, it strengthens the areas of the garment that are likely to wear out fastest.

Since the *huipil* is identical on both sides, it can be worn either way around, so that neither side wears out faster than the other; when a woman is working in the fields, she will sometimes wear her *huipil* inside out to stop the colours fading. When a garment does wear out, the embroidered yoke will be salvaged and attached to a new one, and a zip or a secret inner pocket may be added. The *huipil de cocina* is used for everyday wear and may be tight or loose fitting, short or long, and worn tucked into or over the top of a skirt. A *sobrehuipil* – which is fuller and longer than the *huipil* and not joined at the sides – is worn as an additional over-layer to protect the wearer from the cold.

Young girls dress like their mothers and learn how to weave and embroider from a very early age, generally offering their first *huipil* to a patron saint. This explains why the statues of saints in churches are often dressed in clothes that match those worn by the people of the parish!

The Joyabaj *huipil*, Guatemala

This is a simple but very pretty *huipil* (see overleaf), worn exclusively by the women of Joyabaj. It is short and loosely cut, with whorls of embroidery round the neck – a feature which recalls the *palo volador* performance at the Joyabaj annual festival on 15 August. This is an archaic 'dance' of pre-Columbian origin – Christianized as the 'dance of the Archangel Michael'. Four men wearing masks and disguised as monkeys and angels climb a pole made from a fir trunk. At the top, twenty-five metres above the ground, they secure themselves with a rope harness, spread their arms and launch themselves into space. The ropes unwind from a rotating square structure fixed to the top of the pole, supervised by a musician, and the men fly slowly, head down, performing thirteen rotations before setting foot on the ground again, while the bystanders watch rather nonchalantly – and the women just carry on as if nothing was happening, selling their piping-hot *tamalitos* and embroidering their *huipiles*.

The San Mateo Ixtatán *huipil*, Guatemala

This spectacular *huipil* (see opposite, below) is composed of two layers of fine unbleached cotton and embroidered with huge stars that seem to float in a world of colour. This is a warm and heavy garment, worn over the top of a skirt and completely reversible, and finished with a frill at the neckline.

The San Juan Sacatepéquez *huipil*, Guatemala

Strong colours and an unusual design make this a highly original *huipil* (see overleaf). It has a background of red, mauve and yellow warp stripes in varying widths with a touch of brown derived from natural cotton (*cuyuscate*), and is decorated

with large brocaded motifs – including birds and ears of maize – created by the supplementary weft method. This *huipil* often has a square-cut neckline, edged with green.

The San Antonio Aguas Calientes *huipil*, Guatemala

This very beautiful *huipil* is composed of two wine-coloured panels decorated with numerous figurative motifs embroidered in cross stitch intermixed with geometric motifs brocaded during the weaving. A broad band of flowers and birds is inserted between brightly coloured zigzags or wavy bands and diamond-shaped motifs evoking a row of stars. The trimmings are in green velvet; the square neckline is edged with ribbon and triangles of cloth are appliquéd at the armholes.

Joyabaj *huipil*: two panels joined together, with a round neckline.

Ococingo *huipil*: three panels, with a square neckline.

San Juan Sacatepéquez *huipil*: two panels, with a V-neck.

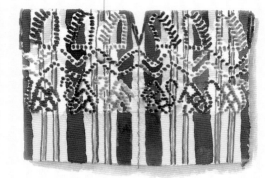

Patzun *huipil*, with a round neck.

This blouse belongs to a little girl from Sololá. It is long, with a split up both front and back to allow greater freedom of movement; it has no collar and the sleeves stop above the wrists. The embroidery – flowers, ears of maize and cat or leopard motifs – has been done by hand and the zigzags at the top of the sleeves symbolize the plumed serpent.

Villagers gathering in Sololá for the festival of the Virgin Mary, men, women and children all dressed in the same fabric. The visual impact is almost overwhelming.

The Aguacatán *huipil*, Guatemala

This *huipil* is composed of two wine-coloured panels and embroidered with birds, flower garlands and the word *corazón* (sweetheart) in cross stitch. It is signed with the embroiderer's initials.

The Nahuala *huipil*, Guatemala

This *huipil* is made up of three panels of cotton. It has a V-neck and a large two-headed bird embroidered on the plastron. On the shoulder is a coyote surmounted by a plumed serpent. The embroidery is in acrylic.

The Todos Santos *huipil*, Guatemala

This *huipil* is made up of three red panels smothered with geometric motifs woven on a backstrap loom. The turquoise yoke is trimmed with interwoven bands of scalloped braid. Blue and purple are currently more fashionable than the traditional red.

The Patzun *huipil*, Guatemala

This wine-coloured *huipil* has narrow stripes of black and white thread. The three panels and the side seams are joined together with an embroidered *randa* using a lustrous mercerized yarn. The neckline is scattered with large stylized flowers, embroidered in running stitch.

The Oxchuc *huipil*, Mexico

The cotton used in Chiapas is finer than Guatemalan cotton. This *huipil* is made up of three widths of cloth striped in white, aubergine and blue and joined together with a multicoloured *randa* that blends into the woven stripes. The neckline is embroidered with bold geometric motifs.

The Sololá blouse, an exception

The women of Sololá wear a top that is more blouse-like than a *huipil* and a fine example of synthesis between Mayan and Western traditions. The cut is reminiscent of Spanish peasant blouses – gathered neckline and tight-fitting wrists – but the cloth itself is locally sourced. Sololá cloth is recognizable by its red, orange, pink, blue and purple stripes interspersed with bands of *jaspe*, the brilliance of the colours and of the *jaspeado* yarn heightened by the addition of embroidery in silver thread, lurex or mercerized cotton. On market days in Sololá, such is the array of coloured fabrics that it becomes difficult to tell the women from the children and the shawls from the bundles.

In some Quiché villages, like San Andrés Sajcabajá, the *huipil* is changing. 'The women have stopped weaving here,' says Antonia sadly. 'Look inside my shop. I sell ready-to-wear blouses. My neighbour buys machine-made lace by the metre and synthetic fabrics, and sews *huipiles* for the whole village – fashionable ones that are short and close-fitting.'

Ixil women *Life in green*

*It almost looks like Switzerland –
green hills all around, the scent of freshly
mown hay, a stream tinkling down in
the valley, cowbells in the fields and a
cheese dairy at the end of the track, run
by Italian émigrés. In fact, we are in the
Acul region of Guatemala, near Nebaj,
the land of the Ixil people.*

*This area suffered badly during
the civil war of the 1980s. Part of the
population fled to Mexico to escape
government reprisals and the scorched-
earth policy adopted by the army. Today,
the memory of those painful years still
lingers, but the scars have long since
faded beneath the lush countryside.*

Ixil women

The women of the Nebaj region are among the most spectacular of the entire Altiplano – a sight worth seeing as they shop in the market, or walk to church or the cemetery on the eve of All Saints' Day.

The local costumes reflect the beauty of the surrounding countryside. The riches of the earth are echoed in the colours of the fabric, the green and red and brown, and the brocade patterns pick up the many birds, animals and plants that inhabit this landscape. Tassels hang from a headdress, framing the wearer's face like flowers, and white embroideries light up the textiles like a ray of sunshine. Heavy, mercerized cotton is used to make the fabrics, and the weaving is dense and teeming with motifs.

The *huipil*: single-sided brocade

Woven using a backstrap loom on a white, green, red or black cotton warp, the tunic or *huipil* is either plain or striped and serves as a backcloth for a host of woven motifs: deer, hummingbird, horse, ear of maize, quetzal and *ceiba*, the Mayans' sacred tree. With single-sided brocade, the design is created by inserting supplementary weft yarns by hand. This gives an embroidered effect, and the supplementary threads appear as loose ends on the reverse side of the fabric.

The *huipil* is made up of two rectangles joined edge to edge in the middle of the back and front, care being taken to match up the patterns on both sides of the join. The dressmaker then cuts a round, oval or square opening for the neck, which she hems and decorates with chain-stitch embroidery in colours that match the weave.

Nebaj women's clothing, Guatemala

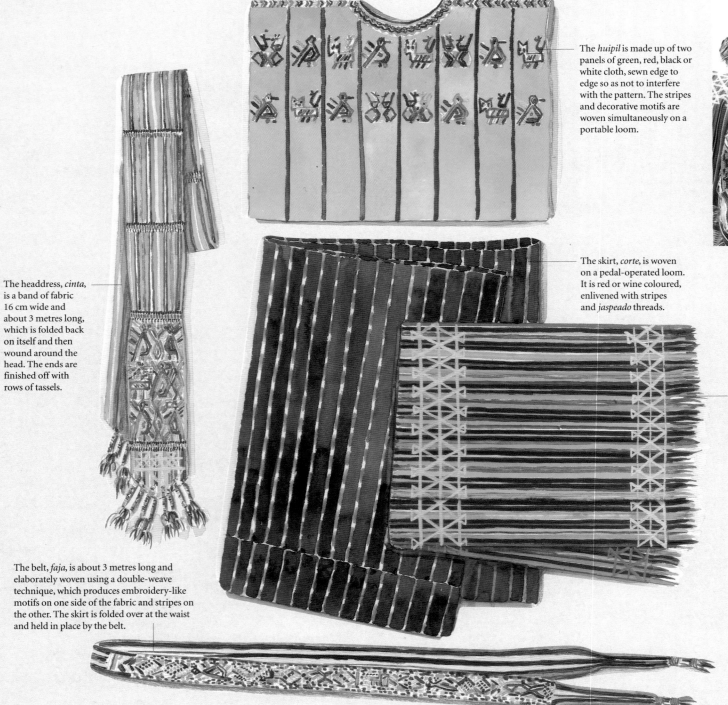

The *huipil* is made up of two panels of green, red, black or white cloth, sewn edge to edge so as not to interfere with the pattern. The stripes and decorative motifs are woven simultaneously on a portable loom.

The skirt, *corte*, is woven on a pedal-operated loom. It is red or wine coloured, enlivened with stripes and *jaspeado* threads.

The headdress, *cinta*, is a band of fabric 16 cm wide and about 3 metres long, which is folded back on itself and then wound around the head. The ends are finished off with rows of tassels.

The woven shawl, *tzute*, is finely striped and embroidered with white geometric designs.

The belt, *faja*, is about 3 metres long and elaborately woven using a double-weave technique, which produces embroidery-like motifs on one side of the fabric and stripes on the other. The skirt is folded over at the waist and held in place by the belt.

Opposite: Detail of a headdress with white embroidery and decorative tassels.

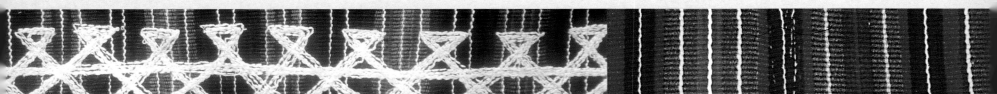

Above: Cristina and Esmeralda have attached their looms to the trunk of a walnut tree, growing at the edge of a meadow, and the colours are creeping up the black cotton warp as their fingers move to and fro.

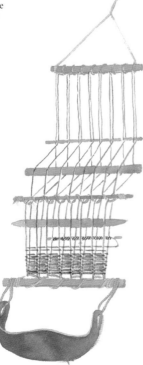

Shawls, belts, headdresses and bags: double-sided brocade

A path leads up to Juana de León's house. Chickens are pecking at grains of maize scattered among stray bits of cotton, and a turkey cock has slipped underneath the loom. In the shelter of the awning, Juana is preparing a piece of weaving and has just warped her multicoloured yarns.

Juana makes long shawls (*rebozos*), and also *tzutes*, *servilletas* (small squares of cloth for wrapping up tortillas), long belts known as *fajas*, and *cintas*, headbands that are over 3 metres long and finished at the ends with large tassels – a rainbow of stripes unfurling under her hands from

morning till night. In typical Nebaj style, she uses a machine to add white scrolls and arabesques in running stitch at the ends of her piece of weaving, and these lighten up the dominant greens.

For a belt or a headdress, which are designed to be seen from both sides, the double-weave technique is used: the principal design appears on the top surface of the cloth, while the supplementary weft yarns form a striped pattern on the reverse. The technique used to weave a bag, or *morral*, is double-sided brocade, which produces an identical design on both sides.

The day continues with a meeting of a local women's association at Doña Magdalena's *posada*. A fine rain is falling over the countryside as the women arrive, each wrapped in a green shawl like a flower in its bud. They gather around the table – and the flowers open up. They have met to discuss credit arrangements and each woman has a twenty-quetzal note in her hand, while the man from the bank makes a list of the contributions. Evening is falling: it is time for Magdalena to light the fire for the *temescal*, the local sauna, a small dark room where the smell of burnt wood catches in your throat, mingling with the scent of aromatic plants. The women slip in through a tiny door, take off their clothes and relax – long enough to work up a good sweat and exchange some gossip.

Left: Diagram of a backstrap loom or belt loom, used for making blouses, shawls and accessories.

Right: A man's bag from Nebaj, woven in a double-sided brocade. A woman is judged on the quality of the bag she weaves for her husband.

The embroidery motif depicting a bird sitting on the back of a horse is a symbol of liberty. It is based on a local legend. According to the story, a young girl falls in love with a handsome young man, but her father disapproves of the match; so the girl changes her lover into a bird in order for him to come to her room unnoticed. The trick is discovered and the bird couple escape on the back of a horse.

Little Ana is dressed like her mother. Her *huipil* is decorated with the motifs of a horse and a hummingbird.

The skirt or *corte*

The one thing I did not see being woven in Nebaj was skirts. For these, I was told, you have to go to the nearby village of Tzalbal.

While all the other elements of local costume are woven by women on a backstrap loom, it is the Tzalbal men who weave the skirts, using a pedal-operated loom and a synthetic red (*corinto*) yarn known as *alemen*. The weft is finely striped in black, yellow and white, interspersed with *jaspeado* yarns. The cloth is only 80 centimetres wide and a 20 centimetre band is added all the way round: the finished skirt is a tube measuring 1 metre by 3 metres, and is held in place with a belt.

Dapper gentlemen *Traditional men's clothing*

It is still possible to find beautifully dressed men as one travels the world. Men with a real sense of style – many of them elderly – who continue to respect ancient customs of dress. But men are more responsive than women to the lure of the West and more and more of them are abandoning their traditional costumes, which are increasingly reserved only for festivals and special occasions.

First to disappear is the traditional shirt, followed by trousers. When these have gone, only the accessories – belts and bags – remain to confer a certain style on an outfit.

In Guatemala, luckily, there are still some twenty villages where men continue to wear all or part of their traditional costume – not as a tourist gimmick but as a feature of everyday life. Exposed to the rigours of the daily grind, to intense sunlight and battering rains, these costumes accompany their wearers like flags, defining their link with a language and a community that are to them a source of pride.

In Mexico and Guatemala, men's dress is a focus for intersecting traditions, both pre-Columbian and Spanish. Men still wear garments of a type worn by their ancestors, including broad belts (*bandas*) reminiscent of Mayan loincloths, sandals (*caites*) like those depicted on ancient stonecarvings, and the *ponchito* or *rodillera*, a woollen skirt, also of pre-Colombian origin.

The straw hat (*sombrero*) was a Spanish import to the region, together with the long-sleeved shirt (*camisa*) with its collar and cuffs, the jacket (*chaqueta*), trousers (*pantalones*) and bag (*morral*).

The result is an audacious blend of styles, materials, colours and embroideries, nowadays often combined with jeans and a baseball cap.

Opposite, from left to right and top to bottom:

A statue of a saint wearing a straw hat.

Men from Todos Santos, leaning against a balustrade.

A smartly dressed man from Joyabaj with his crocheted bag.

The Nebaj jacket. The jacket is Spanish in style, in striped red cloth, with soutache trimming and white embroidery on the cuffs.

Two Man Indians from Todos Santos Cuchumatán wearing black woollen *sobrepantalones*.

Close-up of a pair of trousers from Sololá in embroidered *jaspeado* cloth.

Basilio Ramirez makes trousers for the men of Todos Santos.

A pile of striped cotton on a market stall. It will be used to make shirts and trousers.

In Todos Santos Cuchumatán, it is traditional for men to tie a scarf underneath their straw hat.

Hats on sale in the market.

Dressed in traditionally patterned, short white cotton trousers, a red belt and straw hat, with a bag slung across his shoulder, this man from Santa Catarina Palopó shows that age is no barrier to style.

Left: This little boy is wearing the traditional dress of Todos Santos Cuchumatán, Guatemala – complete in every detail and a perfect counter-example to the erosion of traditional styles.

The traditional shirt (*camisa*) of Todos Santos Cuchumatán, Guatemala.

Below: Woollen *sobrepantalones* from Todos Santos.

White trousers from San Andrés Sajcabaja with decorative stitching and panels overlapping at the waist.

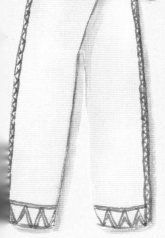

A man from Santiago wearing shorts embroidered with bird motifs.

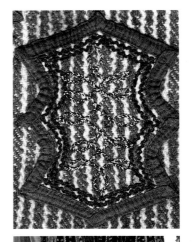

Bird-motif trousers of Santiago Atitlán

To reach Santiago, you have to cross Lake Atitlán in a *cayuco* and disembark at the foot of Tolimán. The lake and the volcano provide a fantastic setting for this village, whose inhabitants, the Tzutujils, are renowned for the elegance of their traditional costume. And in his white knee-length trousers, his red sash and striped shirt, with a hat pushed down on his head, the man waiting to moor the boat does justice to their reputation.

The short trousers are cut from a heavy white cotton, finely striped with black. They are made up of four bands known as *cortecitos*, which are woven on backstrap looms by the women of the neighbouring village of San Pedro de la Laguna. The legs of the trousers are embroidered with a profusion of brightly coloured birds, which appear to be trying to escape from the 'bars' of the fabric.

Sololá, Nahuala and Joyabaj skirts

The *ponchito*, or *rodillera*, is a knee-length woollen skirt, worn over trousers, very fashionable in Sololá and increasingly so in other villages too. The style of weaving, the dimensions of the garment and the method of fastening it are all clues to the wearer's origins. Someone from San Antonio Palopó, for example, will wear his skirt (which measures 140 by 60 cm) rolled over a pair of short trousers, leaving his calves bare. A man from Nahuala will dress almost identically, but the wool of his skirt will be felted, turning the checks to dots of white on black. If a man comes from Joyabaj, however, his *ponchito* will be fringed grey wool folded over his belt to form a double apron.

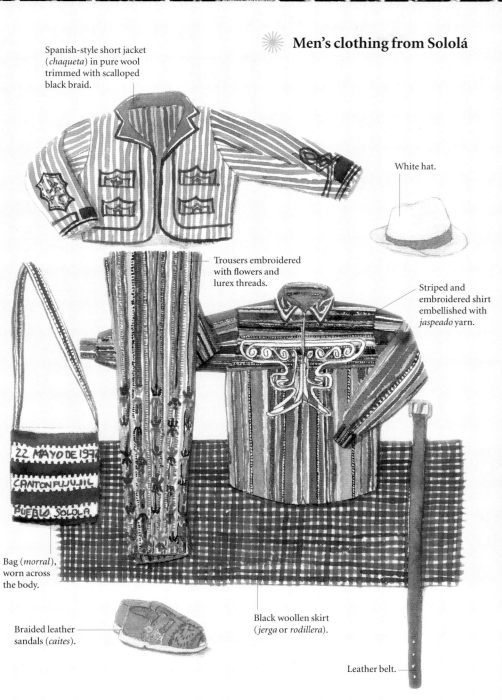

☀ Men's clothing from Sololá

Spanish-style short jacket (*chaqueta*) in pure wool trimmed with scalloped black braid.

White hat.

Trousers embroidered with flowers and lurex threads.

Striped and embroidered shirt embellished with *jaspeado* yarn.

Bag (*morral*), worn across the body.

Braided leather sandals (*caites*).

Black woollen skirt (*jerga* or *rodillera*).

Leather belt.

Baggy trousers and trainers, a loose, untucked shirt and a bag slung across the shoulder create a Western-inspired look. But these two young lads from Todos Santos have also managed to preserve the distinctive features of their own dress culture, along with the traditional colours.

Red trousers of Todos Santos Cuchumatán

The chain of mountains lying along the Mexican border and rising to 3,500 metres is known as Sierra de los Cuchumatanes. It encircles the region of Todos Santos, cutting it off from the rest of Guatemala and making it unusually damp and cold. In this grey and misty place, the figures of the local men stand out like brilliant blue and red flowers.

It is in the market that we get the first glimpse of the traditional Todos Santos trousers – or rather, the piles of red and white striped cloth that go to make them. The trousers can be found in finished form at the *sastrería típico*, the shop belonging to the local tailor, Basilio Ramírez. Todos Santos trousers are a good example of how clothing styles can evolve: the traditional version of the garment, woven on a backstrap loom, has bowed to Western influence by borrowing style details – such as stitching, rivets, pockets, loops and flies – from denim jeans, while at the same time preserving its most specific feature – the bright fabric, with its huge range of stripes, manufactured in small local factories.

The Todos Santos shirt (*camisa*) is also a perfect example of how two traditions can come together: it is Western in cut and made from a mass-produced striped cotton, but the wearer's wife decorates it with a handmade collar and cuffs that match her own *huipil*.

Over their red trousers, the men wear a second pair of trousers made from black wool and known as *sobrepantalones*. These are split up the front of the leg and fastened with large white buttons, and are thought to have been originally Spanish in influence. A jacket or blouson is also worn for warmth, along with a straw hat decorated with studs and brocade ribbon, and sometimes a headscarf, or *tzute*, tied beneath the hat.

Above left: 'You must go there, if only to see the men!' That was what I had been told. And so, on a damp, grey Sunday, I meet Juan. He is dressed in the traditional tunic of the village of San Martín Sacatepéquez: cut from finely striped white cotton, it is long and collarless and has brocaded sleeves sewn on. His trousers come down to his calves and are decorated at the bottom with a panel of embroidery. His red belt is tied at the back, and he is wearing a straw hat jammed down on his head and a pair of large, heavy boots.

Above right: At San Andrés Sajcabaja, a man rides up on his horse looking like a cowboy from the Wild West. He is wearing trousers crossed over at the waist, with a wide red belt, a Western shirt, a stiff straw hat with a broad brim and a pair of boots, and carrying a traditional crocheted cotton bag.

Right: Pedro sets off, wearing his *capixay* (whose sleeves are too narrow to get his arms through), and a long red belt, over a red shirt with embroidered sleeves and collar, and a pair of white trousers. His bag (which he crocheted himself), his small straw hat and the shawl (*tzute*) over his shoulder complete an outfit so effortlessly stylish it could have come straight from the pages of a book. And what a bonus when that smile lights up his lined face!

Overleaf, from left to right: Circular embroidered motifs on a Joyabaj *rodillera* or man's skirt; a man from Nahuala; a checked wool *rodillera*, seen in close-up; close-up showing *jaspeado* yarns and embroidery on trousers from Sololá.

The San Juan Atitlán *capixay*

The village of San Juan Atitlán is perched at a height of 3,000 metres, in the hills of Cuchumatanes. 'To get back to San Juan from the market at Todos Santos, it's a good three hours' walk, on muddy paths. So I don't hang around,' says Pedro, looking at his watch. He barely gives me time to take a photo before he strides off, adjusting his *capixay*, a rectangular brown woollen garment resembling a monk's habit, whose narrow sleeves flap up and down on his shoulders like wings.

Well-matched couples

Perhaps it's a question of like attracting like – although we cannot, of course, assume that dressing alike means getting along all the time. Does a shared life create a shared sense of style, or are these people simply cut from the same cloth?

Right: San Juan Atitlán: José and Magdalena. They are sitting on the edge of the pavement, just waiting patiently for the wedding party to emerge from the church. Birds are twittering on José's trousers and their brothers and sisters are hovering round the white flowers on Magdalena's violet-coloured *huipil.* Skirt and shirt complement one another, her pink stripes matching his blue checks and even the turquoise of the wall behind them. José and Magdalena are the perfectly matched couple, half smiling, modest but also conscious of how good they look.

Left: Sololá: Juan and Maria. It is 15 August, the feast day of the Virgin Mary, and there is a carnival atmosphere in Sololá. Families from nearby villages are pouring into the town. This old couple are on their way to church. When the service is over, they will follow the *cofradias* (confraternities) as they process through the steep streets. Juan and Maria have the deeply lined faces of mountain-dwellers. Every detail of Juan's outfit is traditional: shirt, jacket, *ponchito,* trousers, hat, bag, leather belt and the red *tzute* tied around his waist. (Through the gap in his shirt, we can see a hint of blue t-shirt.) Maria is looking just as smart as her husband, wearing her *tzute* folded on top of her head and a black cardigan to protect her from the morning chill. The little white dots scattered over Juan's black *ponchito* are echoed by the black and white *jaspe* in Maria's skirt: the effect is a bit like partridge feathers.

Opposite, above left: Todos Santos: Jovanna and Marcello. These two share several things: they seem to enjoy their food (they are sipping iced water with a bit of fruit syrup in it) and are very conscious of their appearance. Their hats are identical, straw trimmed with studs and braid.

Opposite, below left: Todos Santos: Diego and Antonia. This couple have walked from their *pueblito* to the market at Todos Santos Cuchumatán. They are dressed in identical colours: red, pink, black, turquoise and white. Diego's shirt collar, woven by his wife, is in the same yarn as her *huipil* and the patterns are also the same. Her blouse is trimmed with crocheted braid and velvet, and a triangle of the same shade of turquoise can be seen in the opening of Diego's shirt. Their belts are woven in the same bright red striped with white, and the vibrant red, pink and turquoise provide a striking contrast with the dark indigo of her skirt and his woollen *sobrepantalones.*

Nebaj: Antonio and Martina. This couple are in Nebaj on business, but decide to stay on for the village festival. Antonio is holding the Polaroid print I have just given him and intends to pin it to the wall at home, between a horseshoe and an *ex voto* picture. Although his clothes are relatively plain, Antonio's bag (*chim* in Quiché) – which he tells me he crocheted himself – picks up the colours of Martina's *huipil*, turban and shawl and looks almost neon-bright.

The blues of Lake Atitlán

This turquoise caldera nestles in a hollow, ringed by a trio of majestic volcanoes, Tolimán, Atitlán and San Pedro, and the best way to discover the variety of local costumes is to jump in a little boat and sail from village to village, around the perimeter of the lake. Red used to be the predominant colour in Santa Catarina and San Antonio Palopó, but today the villagers wear the colours of the lake itself – turquoise and mauve – while the primary inspiration for Santiago Atitlán's embroiderers seems to be the flocks of birds that frequent its shores.

Above: Young girls from the village of Santa Catarina.
Opposite: Santa Catarina fishermen, the lake and the volcano. Santiago Atitlán lies in the far distance.

Santa Catarina Palopó

Perched precariously on the side of the mountain, with its feet in the lake, Santa Catarina Palopó boasts little in the way of arable land. The men rely on fishing, and the women weave and embroider incessantly, supplying the shops in Panajachel.

San Antonio Palopó

San Antonio Palopó huddles round its white church, surrounded by terraces where maize, beans, onions and aniseed are grown for sale in the market at Sololá. Until 1960, there was no road to the village and the only way to reach it was by boat.

I have been admiring Rafael's shirt and, at his invitation, I follow him through a maze of narrow streets that leads us to the tiniest of workshops.

On a tiny terrace, Antonio's entire family are busy spinning, weaving and winding cotton onto bobbins. The older boy is making tassels, the younger one winding spools of thread; Marta is preparing a warp for a scarf, and Antonella is weaving one of the narrow blue bands that the local women wear wrapped around their braids. Threads of cotton stretch in all directions like a spider's web drying in the wind.

The striped cotton of Rafael's shirt was woven and cut at home: the sleeves and body of the shirt are intentionally woven in different stripes. The collar is a rectangular band that has been sewn on and reinforced with brightly coloured stripes of embroidery in satin stitch. The front of the shirt is made up of two sections of cloth joined along the selvedge. Sometimes these are fixed together with stitching, so that the shirt has to be pulled on over the head, or alternatively they may have a zip fastening. Cuffs, pockets and buttons seem to be regarded as an irrelevance in San Antonio Palopó, where everything seems to be in a shade of turquoise: men's clothing, women's clothing, the lake, of course, and even the walls of the buildings.

Santiago Atitlán

This little village nestles at the foot of the volcano of Tolimán, on an old lava flow, and is an important religious centre – hence the gorgeous Mayan costumes that cloth the wooden statues in the church. It is also here, in Santiago Atitlán, and in the village of San Pedro de la Laguna, that all the boats one sees crisscrossing the waters of the lake are built, using avocado wood.

Men's trousers in Santiago Atitlán are richly embroidered (see page 166), and the village is also famous for its ikat or *jaspe* technique (see pages 130–33). It is also a tradition (which is now dying out) for women to wear a *tocayal*, a red ribbon about ten metres long with brocade patterns at the end, which they wind around their head like a brilliant halo.

Panajachel

It is to Panajachel that the boats, or *cayucos*, come from the surrounding villages, laden with produce for sale in the market at Sololá. The village has become quite a tourist attraction, but is still very charming, with its pretty church and neighbouring streets bordered with hibiscus and bougainvilleas. And the little morning fleamarket is certainly worth a visit – an absolute treasure trove where you will find piles of old silk *rebozos* from Totonicapán, *huipiles* from Patzún, *cintas*, *bolses*, and more.

The light too is magnificent here, and the banks of the lake are planted with tamarisks and willows, which offer shelter to the ruddy duck (*pato zambullidor*) and migrant birds such as flycatchers.

CARIBBEAN SEA

El Porvenir

Gardi Sugdub

Rio
Azúcar

SAN BLAS ISLANDS

KUNA YALA

KUNA

SERRANÍA DE SAN BLAS

Ailigandi
Achutupu
Mamitupu

COLÓN

CHAGRES
NATIONAL
PARK

PANAMA CANAL

LAKE
ALAJUELA

LAKE
GATÚN

Chepo

PANAMA

LAKE
BAYANO

SERRANÍA DE DARIÉN

PANAMA CITY

SERRANÍA DE MAJE

Cañazas

GULF OF PANAMA

EMBERA

DARIÉN

CHOCOL

Los Monos

COLOMBIA

Panama
The Kuna archipelago

Panama is rather like a hammock strung between North and South America. A hammock in which a beautiful American Indian woman – a Kuna woman – is swinging to and fro as the waves of the Caribbean beat gently on the shore.

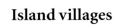

Island villages

The journey from Panama City takes us by plane, over the tropical canopy, then by boat to Kuna Yala, the spectacular region of the Kuna people – a string of coral islands, complete with sandy beaches and coconut palms, that seem to float like a mirage on the turquoise waters of the lagoon.

There are some three hundred and sixty islands in the San Blas archipelago – a partially autonomous region – but of these, only forty are inhabited. The islands look like giant sea turtles, the close-set rows of palm-roofed huts like the overlapping scales of a shell, with here and there a mango tree, breadfruit tree or coconut palm adding a touch of green to this mass of dwellings.

A labyrinth of colours

Like a butterfly

In the damp tropical heat, the slender figure of a Kuna woman slips between the bamboo huts like a brightly coloured butterfly. The woman settles on a stool at the entrance to one of the huts and takes up her workbox.

Then other butterflies seem to emerge from her basket, in the form of rectangles of brilliant-coloured fabric, bobbins of thread, and little pieces of cut-out cloth used to decorate a woman's blouse. Known as molas, *these are the miniature works of art that the San Blas islands are famous for.*

Kuna women may be slightly built, but there is nothing slight about their roles in this matriarchal society, in which women are free to choose their husbands and the birth of a daughter to continue the family line is regarded as an event to be celebrated. A girl's transition into adulthood is marked by a series of ceremonies, beginning with the festival of Ico Inna, the 'Festival of the Needle', when she has her nose pierced and a gold ring inserted. The festival of Inna Suit then marks the onset of puberty and is an important rite of passage attended by several days of celebrations. The young girl receives the name that she will now keep for life and has her hair cut (as the 'Scissors Song' is sung), short at the nape, with a fringe left at the front. Her first menstrual cycle will be celebrated at the festival of Inna Muustiki, and at her marriage a woman decorates her arms and legs with beaded ornaments and covers her head with a red headscarf.

But customs change and deviations from this standard dress code do occur. Women studying or working in Panama City, for example, wear their traditional costumes only when they return to their island, and schoolgirls swap their uniforms for Kuna garments each day when they come home from school.

Opposite: Teresa Morales was born on 23 January 1923 and is seen here, sitting in a doorway, sewing a *mola*. Like the majority of *mu* (grandmothers and great-grandmothers), she is very image-conscious and wears a heavy gold nose ring. Teresa wanted to be photographed with her pet parakeet – which matches the green in her skirt – and also insisted on removing her glasses.

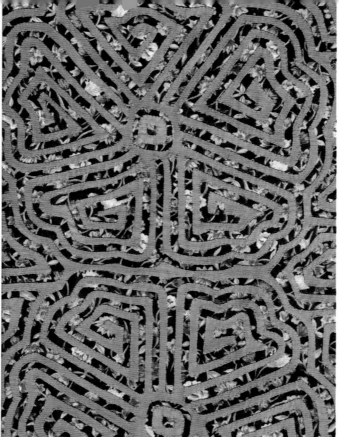

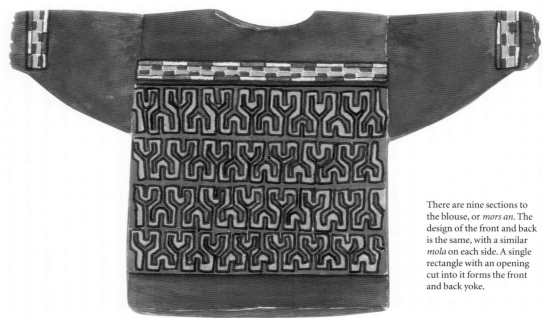

There are nine sections to the blouse, or *mors an*. The design of the front and back is the same, with a similar *mola* on each side. A single rectangle with an opening cut into it forms the front and back yoke.

Antonia is washing her grandson using a calabash (the hollow shell of a gourd). She tells me: '*I feel more comfortable wearing my wrap as a dress.*' Slim and short-haired, she looks like a very youthful and lively grandmother.

Opposite, top left: Elvira lives on the island of Achutupo. She has smeared her cheekbones with the pulp of a red fruit, *achiote* – whether for appearances' sake or as a protective measure is unclear – and her cheeks are glowing in the light of the setting sun. The Kunas harvest their medicinal plants from the jungle that grows near the coast.

Opposite, top right: Praolina is 38 and lives on the island of Ailigandi. She works as a cook on Dad Ibe and crosses the lagoon each morning in a pirogue. '*Like my mother and my grandmother, I draw a thin black line down the middle of my nose with jagua. It's a plant that grows in the forest. You crush it and as it oxidizes it stains your skin. I do it every few weeks.*'

Women with long, aquiline noses are regarded as beautiful among the Kuna people: the gold ring and black line draw attention to the nose and emphasize its length. Drawing on the face is probably a throwback to the days when the whole body was covered with tattoos, which may in turn have inspired the graphic style of the first *molas*.

Right: Beaded leg and arm ornaments.

A Kuna from head to toe

A Kuna woman is forever tying and untying her red scarf, her *muswe*; if it starts to slip, she ties it on again; she unties it to wipe her face and drapes it round her head, tucking it behind her ears.

The *muswe* is a Caribbean variant of the bandanna. Cut from imported cloth, bought for two or three dollars in the little village stores or in Panama City's Avenida Central, it is made up of two squares with raw edges, printed with traditional yellow patterns with a border and a central motif.

As a skirt, a Kuna woman wears a *sabured*, a wrap or sarong in dark blue or green printed with geometric motifs. Depending on age and personal taste, the *sabured* can be worn long or short.

Wini, or *canilleras* in Spanish, are ornaments for the arms and legs, made up of tiny plastic and glass beads strung on cotton thread in a complex grid pattern. The ornaments take several hours to weave and the women change them every two or three weeks. The motifs range from simple two-coloured stripes to Greek key motifs using three or four colours, which echo the interlacing designs of the *molas*, as well as the local basketweaving designs and the palm fans (*habánicos*) made by the men.

Kuna women are fond of ornaments of all kinds – necklaces, earrings, nose rings, finger rings. Many of them still paint a black line down their nose highlight the symmetry of the face, but the tradition of nose piercing is changing. Over three generations of women, you may well see the grandmother wearing a gold nose ring, the mother two little gold balls instead of a ring, and the daughter no nose ring at all – though she may have her ears pierced instead. Plastic necklaces are also replacing gold ones, adding a touch of extra colour to an outfit.

Kuna blouses

Molas themselves are still made of cotton, but the blouses that feature them are now made from synthetic materials, which are apparently prized for their softness and brilliance. 'Never mind if it's warmer,' I hear, 'it dries quicker!'

The Kuna blouse, *mors an*, is made up of nine sections. It once had shoulder yokes, but these have now disappeared, and the former short sleeves have been replaced by puff sleeves that come down to the elbow.

The blouse may be sewn either by hand or by machine, but the *mola* is always handmade. A blouse without a *mola* is unthinkable, whereas a *mola* without a blouse is an artefact designed merely with the tourist in mind. When a blouse has become a bit tired, the *mola* is taken off and sewn on to a new one or sold, either alone or as part of a pair.

Zigzag braid and gold ribbons have gradually replaced the bands of decorative appliqué that used to be positioned above the yoke and on the elbows – after all, fashions change. And from Asia to Central America, if the choice is between cotton and lurex, a young girl will simply not hesitate. Nothing attracts the boys more than glitter and shine! We may bemoan the loss of a beautiful tradition, but the Chinese braid manufacturers have no cause to mourn.

Tilsia Fernández lives on the island of Ailigandi. She is seen here sitting in front of her house, next to a tray of drying maize. *'I'll sell you this blouse, if you want,'* she says. *'I've put on weight and it's too small for me now. The design is called* naku mor. *It's based on the paddles which weavers used to compress the cotton yarns when they were making a hammock. Only old Felicia makes hammocks now. Today, people buy them ready made from the Colombians who regularly come here in their boats – floating shops, more like – with their groceries and their cooking pots and their hardware. The design also represents the paddles from a dug-out.'*

Opposite: Close-up of the paddle design described above by Tilsia Fernández.

The *mola*, a textile journey

Reverse appliqué

The pouring rain has stopped, for now, and the sun is beating down. Suddenly bumping into a woman wearing a mola, *at a bend in the path, is like encountering a vision from another world.*

A mola *is the key item in a Kuna woman's outfit. She wears one every day and she is always busy making more of them:* molas *are the key to her identity, to what is most 'Kuna' about her. And these brilliant motifs that express her life and dreams and beliefs in images are also miniature works of art that have attracted the interest of collectors and ethnologists alike.*

Right: Elena working on a *mola*, on the island of Achutupo. The design represents an ant's nest. The top layer of fabric is maroon, the middle one yellow, and the bottom one – revealed in the very centre of the spiralling curves – blue.

The *mola* technique

A *mola* is a rectangular piece of cloth measuring about 30 cm by 40 cm, and forms the front or back of a woman's blouse. It is made using reverse appliqué, a technique which is practised in many other parts of the world: the women of the Hmong tribes in Laos and Vietnam and the Miao in China use it to decorate collars, belts, bags and baby-carriers, and the Banjara nomads, in India, and the people of Sind, in Pakistan, embellish their quilts with reverse appliqué in white on white.

To create a piece of reverse appliqué, several layers of cloth are laid one on top of the other and tacked together. A design is drawn on the top layer and then cut with a pair of pointed scissors to reveal the fabric beneath. The point of the needle is then used to turn down the edges of the cut material and the rolled edges are hemmed with small stitches. Only the simplest equipment is required – some pieces of plain cotton fabric, matching thread, a fine needle and a pair of scissors – and nothing is wasted, since the snippets of cloth cut from one *mola* will be used to decorate the next one.

The more layers there are, the more colours, and in theory the more beautiful the finished effect. In fact, two-colour *molas* can also be very beautiful, although the current fashion is for multicoloured work. In addition to the two or three principal layers, a small piece of a contrasting colour can be slipped in between two layers and the colour revealed by cutting. Complementary details can also be added, including some colourful embroidery: when she is designing a *mola*, a Kuna woman is free to sew whatever she likes.

Above: Praolina and Jovanna make *molas* in any moment of free time they can snatch – and take advantage of the opportunity for a chat. Their short skirts reveal their slim legs.

'We always sew two molas *at the same time: the one on the front is a copy of the one on the back. They are never exactly alike, and the best one always goes on the back of the blouse because it's the side where you see it best.'*

Mola symbolism: drawing on life

Molas can be read like a book: what they depict are the elements of everyday life, past and present, the dreams, fears, hopes and aspirations of their creators. They are like storybooks, rich and detailed, that take us off on a journey.

We can group them roughly by subject matter, but it is worth bearing in mind that the same motif may inspire quite different interpretations – literal in one case, symbolic in another.

Some very geometric *molas* appear to take their inspiration from nature – from the outline of a coral reef, the shape of a sea urchin or woven palm leaves, the intersecting streets in a village, ridges in the sand, a rainbow or the contour lines of a mountain.

Molas can also represent stylized images of animals: the tracks left by a hermit crab, for instance, a skate, two pelicans, two eels, a sea turtle, four monkeys, a dolphin, a falcon or a snake. Or they may take their subject from the plant world, representing four gourds, for example, a coconut palm, a flower, a pepper or a mango tree. The imagery may relate to everyday objects – pirogues, umbrellas, hammocks, communal houses (*onmaket nega*) – or to more abstract concepts, such as thunder, the moon, whirlwinds, sickness. *Molas* may even find inspiration beyond Panama's borders, from Father Christmas, for example, or a cartoon character.

I gave a Kuna woman a postcard showing a view of Paris, and she told me she would copy the picture onto a *mola* – such is the power of inspiration!

A Kuna woman displays her handiwork in the Casco Viejo quarter, facing the skyscrapers of Panama City – but a world away from them.

Whether you're getting from one island to another or going fishing, you need a fair wind and a pirogue like this one, rigged with a makeshift sail. Made from old clothes sewn together, it looks more like a work of art than a sail. Large-scale fishing is forbidden in the lagoon, which is rich in fish, octopus, crayfish and crabs.

Molas: a passion and a business

Molas have given rise to a flourishing trade that is utterly imbued with the Kuna Indian culture and by selling their handiwork, Kuna women gain a level of financial independence. They are passionate about their *molas* and the family also relies on them as a source of income. Here, then, is a situation that many women can only dream of, combining creative satisfaction with a means of earning a living and also achieving recognition for the quality of one's work.

Molas sell for between 5 and 30 dollars and bring in enough money to cover a family's daily living expenses and pay for the children's studies and school uniform – although, inevitably, some of the profits have to be ploughed back, to pay for fabric, thread, needles or a sewing machine and spectacles for those who can afford them.

The men in the family earn a living from fishing for crayfish, octopus and crabs, which end up on restaurant menus in Panama City or dished up for the tourists. The work is seasonal and the family also supplement their income by growing and selling coconuts.

From left to right and top to bottom: Mountain *mola*. Village streets *mola*. Fish *mola*. Flower *mola*. Two birds *mola*. Hammocks *mola*. Two falcons *mola*. Cat *mola*: this mola represents a cat surrounded by greenery and framed by two flower buds. There are two layers, maroon at the top, green below. The pink and black fabric of the cat's body is appliquéd, as are the multicoloured motifs inside the body. These may represent the bones of a fish swallowed by the cat, while the coloured stitching suggests the cat's fur. Labyrinth *mola*.

Romania
Maramures and Bukovina

Cradled in the foothills of the Carpathians, these lush valleys remain unchanged and life goes on as it always has. We could be in a painting by Brueghel: people are making hay and milking cows, hoeing and spinning, shearing, harnessing and harvesting, or sitting quietly in the stillness of a wooden church. But this is not 16th-century Flanders: this is the present day in Maramures: pronounced with a soft hushing sound, 'Maramuresh'.

Further to the east lie the rolling grasslands of Bukovina, and a melting pot of diverse traditions, where Romanians, Hutsuls, Ukrainians, Poles, Lipovans, Moldovans and Romany tinsmiths and coppersmiths all come together.

Experiencing Romania is like burying one's head in a pillow smelling of hay; it is like going back to childhood and rediscovering the real taste of apples and the crunch of snow, panfuls of soup simmering on the stove, painted Easter eggs and carnival masks, the smell of horse dung and the clatter of hooves. And here in Romania's hidden valleys are the last of those treasures that Europe has so wilfully forgotten or discarded or stuffed behind glass – the last traditional folk costumes.

They call it 'our costume', *portul nostra*, and they all wear it – Constantin, on his way to the sawmill, Viorika and Lucia, shopping in the market, and Sandor and Ion, going to buy spirits from the local distiller. The traditional costume is part of everyday life here, thanks to the peasants, and to the parish priest who assembles his congregation for the Sunday service, and to the friendly folk who enjoy sharing meals and celebrating together and will dress for the occasion in their most glorious attire.

Romanian folk costume survives in many forms, whether traditional or improvised, handed down or adapted: it is flamboyant, authentic, and improbably anachronistic. We only have to think back to those fashion collections full of Romanian blouses, fringed shawls and gypsy skirts, or the flowers and ribbons that brighten our city streets. While Romanians submitted to the Ceausescu straitjacket, their national dress styles flourished beyond the borders of their country.

Romania is a place we associate with nostalgia: with melodies played on a gypsy violin in Maramures, with evenings spent drinking plum brandy with the locals, or with a folk band playing at a wedding celebration or escorting a funeral procession in Bukovina. And the local dress, like the music, is imbued with nostalgia: this is one of the last traditional costumes still to be worn in Europe.

 Living traditions

Romanian peasant blouses

While the stallholders are setting out their produce in the covered market, Michaela does the rounds, offering a taste of her telemea (a cheese, rather like feta) to anyone prepared to try it.

Catalina – whom we meet on the road to Suceava – is dressed so stylishly she could have stepped straight out of the pages of a 1970s fashion magazine. Every detail is just right: the Slavic blouse and coral necklace, the sheepskin gilet, gathered black sateen skirt and headscarf. Catalina's lined face and hands, however, prove that she is the genuine article: a real Romanian country woman, not just a city-dweller masquerading in peasant costume.

Blouses from Maramures and Bukovina

The market at Sighet is full of round-faced women selling apples and plums who look as wholesome and appealing as the fruit from their farms. It feels as if they had stepped straight out of the markets of our childhood. With their rough hands and their round faces, their full figures swathed in aprons, and scarves tied under their chin, they conjure up all the images of a lost rural paradise.

Some of these women – like Ionela, who sells paprika – are wearing the *camasa* or *camesoi*, the blouse for which Romania is famous.

The most popular type of blouse in Maramures has a yoke and a square neckline. It is delicately trimmed with braid and has a white lace edging around the armholes and on the yoke and cuffs. In Bukovina, the women prefer Slavic-style blouses – a style which the artist Matisse (an enthusiastic collector of textiles) also seems to have favoured, since he did a number of drawings and paintings of women wearing garments of this kind.

The other key element of traditional costume here is the other is the headscarf. Widows wear black scarves, while a brighter version is made from fine wool with a large floral print and a fringe. Few country women are to be seen without a scarf, whether they tie it under their chin, to create a rather severe look, or swathe it around their neck. It provides a key – clearly understood by anyone who knows the code – to social status, age and identification with a particular village or community. In the words of one old Romanian woman, 'A woman's hair should no longer see the sun once she has worn the marriage crown!'

Above: Dressed all in black, Anita has come to market to sell her black hen.

Opposite, above left: Bags like this one are traditionally carried by country people in Romania. The bags are handmade from checked cloth and have a woven or braided shoulder strap.

Opposite, above centre: Ionela is wearing a blouse with a square neckline. Her freshly ground paprika is a sought-after commodity here.

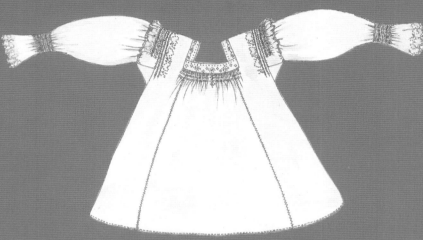

A typical blouse from Maramures, the *latitare* is sewn by hand and trimmed along the seams with openwork embroidery, known as *cheite*. There is smocking on the shoulders and at the wrists, with white stitching to hold the gathers in place. The blouse can be either short or long (in which case it is tucked into a gathered skirt or an apron).

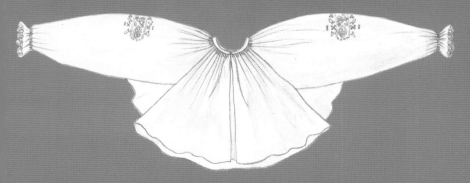

A Slavic-style blouse, part of the traditional costume of several Eastern European countries. It is loose fitting, with a gathered neckline that fastens with a drawstring, and is often embroidered on the front and sleeves. The absence of armholes makes it very comfortable to wear, and it can also be worn with the drawstring ties loosened. This style of blouse was featured in the collections of Yves Saint-Laurent.

An Orthodox Sunday

A sea of woolly sheepskins

In a valley in Maramures, little groups of men and women are drifting towards Poienile Izei's charming wooden church. The priest bangs a wooden beam hanging in the church porch, which is his way of summoning the faithful. Danuta has picked a few flowers from her garden for decoration, and Constantin and Dimitriu come charging out from behind the apple trees. Grandmothers are arriving with their granddaughters in tow: dressed in their flowery skirts, starched blouses and headscarves, the little girls (who have come for a holiday on the farm) look a little like dolls. After the service, the congregation gathers in the cemetery, in the shade of some plum trees, to share rounds of paprika sausage, grapes and *tuica*, the local spirit.

Bukovina is several valleys to the east, the other side of the Prislop Pass. Dragan is harnessing his horse and cart so that he can accompany the Sunday procession. He tightens his *chimir*, the broad leather belt worn by country folk, and throws his gilet – in reversed sheepskin edged with fox fur – around his shoulders, striking a pose for the camera, knowing full well how smart he looks. Inside the church, there is a whole sea of soft woolly sheepskins, smothered in embroidery, and row upon row of floral headscarves.

Maramures's wooden churches, the majority of which date from the 18th century, are real architectural gems and carefully maintained. The interior is decorated with murals, icons and wall-hangings, and smells of wood and incense, creating a very peaceful atmosphere.

Dragan posing in front of his Moldavian home, a large wooden house decorated with fretwork. He is wearing a reversed sheepskin, a broad leather belt with little pockets in it and a felt hat. 'When it rains or snows,' he explains, 'I wear my gilet inside out to protect the embroidery.'

Embroidery on a reversed sheepskin gilet.

A gilet, *boanda*, in reversed sheepskin. A sheepskin gilet or coat is the traditional garment of the Carpathian Mountains, worn by Hungarians, Poles, Ukrainians, Slovaks and Afghans. The raw sheepskin has to be scoured and softened, and then oiled to make it water-repellent.

Haymaking, spinning and felting

All things in their season

Summer

Juliana, Adela and Lucia are sitting on a bench by the house – where they can gossip and spin and knit, while keeping half an eye on what is going on in the street. This is a common sight in Romania and one that encapsulates the sociable nature of village life.

It is late afternoon and extremely peaceful. There are wafts of scent from the lime trees and a jingling of bells announces the return of carts loaded with hay from the fields.

Anton in a traditional shirt and straw hat, looking pretty pleased with himself.

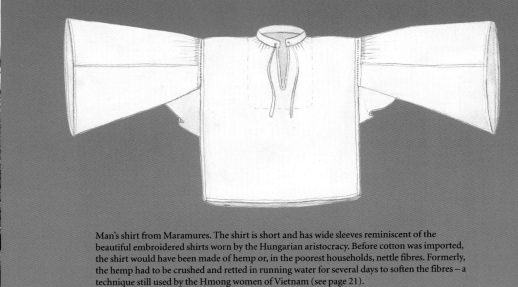

Man's shirt from Maramures. The shirt is short and has wide sleeves reminiscent of the beautiful embroidered shirts worn by the Hungarian aristocracy. Before cotton was imported, the shirt would have been made of hemp or, in the poorest households, nettle fibres. Formerly, the hemp had to be crushed and retted in running water for several days to soften the fibres – a technique still used by the Hmong women of Vietnam (see page 21).

Autumn

The autumn mist envelops the Botiza valley and sweet woody smells mingle with the smell of plums from the bubbling still.

Once the wool has been spun and wound into skeins, it is time to start weaving aprons and checked bags and rugs, and to make the woollen cloth for felting.

In Maramures, the apron (*catrinta* or *zadii*) is a simple rectangle whose colours and striping vary from village to village. It is worn over a white cotton underskirt (*poale*) and is in fact a double apron – like those of the Hmong and Yao women of South East Asia (see pages 12–13) – with one section at the front and another at the back.

This is the felting season. The women take their weaving to the fulling mill (*piua*), which is powered by water, or if there is no mill, to a tank by the river, where they felt the woven wool in cold water. They need to be quick and get the job done before the first frosts.

Felting increases the thickness of wool and also makes it water-repellent, and is a technique practised all round the world – to make berets in the Basque country, boots in Russia, slippers in Sweden, skirts in Chiapas, and a covering for yurts in Mongolia. The practice of felting predates weaving and may have been inspired by the observation of how sheep's wool naturally becomes matted during the moulting season.

Right: Juliana sitting in front of her house in Maramures and spinning wool from a distaff (*furca de tors*). *'It's the men's job to do the shearing,'* she says. *'They start when the days get warmer and the first tufts of wool get spiked on the bushes. The sheep go up to the mountain pastures on St George's Day, in late April, and come back down on St Dimitriu's Day, in late October.'*

Left: These shoes, known as *opinca*, have an almost medieval look They are made of a rectangular leather sole with the edges turned up on top of the foot and secured with narrow straps. Like the gilet and the coat, *opinca* are worn by both men and women. They are summer footwear (boots are preferred in winter) and an indispensable part of the traditional costume worn for festivals.

Another technique for felting wool involves placing the cloth over a layer of mesh, splashing it with hot water and beating it for hours. As it is beaten and kneaded, the cloth becomes compacted and thickened. Felted wool is traditionally used in Tyrolean costumes and is associated with folk costumes generally, but it is currently quite fashionable. It has the advantage that it can be cut without fraying and sewn edge to edge, eliminating the need for a hem or concealed seams.

Modern felted fabrics have a particularly soft texture, combining the hang of traditional woollen cloth with the elasticity of a knit, and have found their way into contemporary fashion collections.

As winter approaches, the felted wool is used to make coats and gilets – women's work again. The *suman* (coat) and the *pieptar* (gilet) are worn by both men and women, but while the gilet is still a popular garment, the heavy coat has become something of an anachronism and tends to be reserved for Christmas festivals.

Right: When he was asked why he was wearing a felt gilet in the middle of summer, Bogdan replied rather curtly: 'I wouldn't be without it. I shall wear it till the day I die.'

The *aba* or *suman* is a long, generously cut winter coat of felted wool in a natural shade (grey, black, beige or white), trimmed with braids and with felt and leather appliqué. The front flap wraps around and is secured with a belt made of leather or embroidered wool. Bias inserts give the coat extra width, and the felting makes it relatively waterproof.

The coat has a square collar that can be turned into a hood, and is usually worn slung round the shoulders, as a cape, because the stiffness of the fabric makes it awkward to put on. Shepherds and herdsmen wear it to protect them from the elements and the coat can also serve as a bedcover or mattress – and eventually as a shroud. Over the border in Hungary, the same heavy wool coat is smothered with embroidery and known as a *cifraszur*, a key element in Hungarian men's dress.

The *pieptar* or gilet is made of pure wool trimmed with leather or corduroy velvet, but is gradually being replaced by a lighter padded version, made from synthetic fibres.

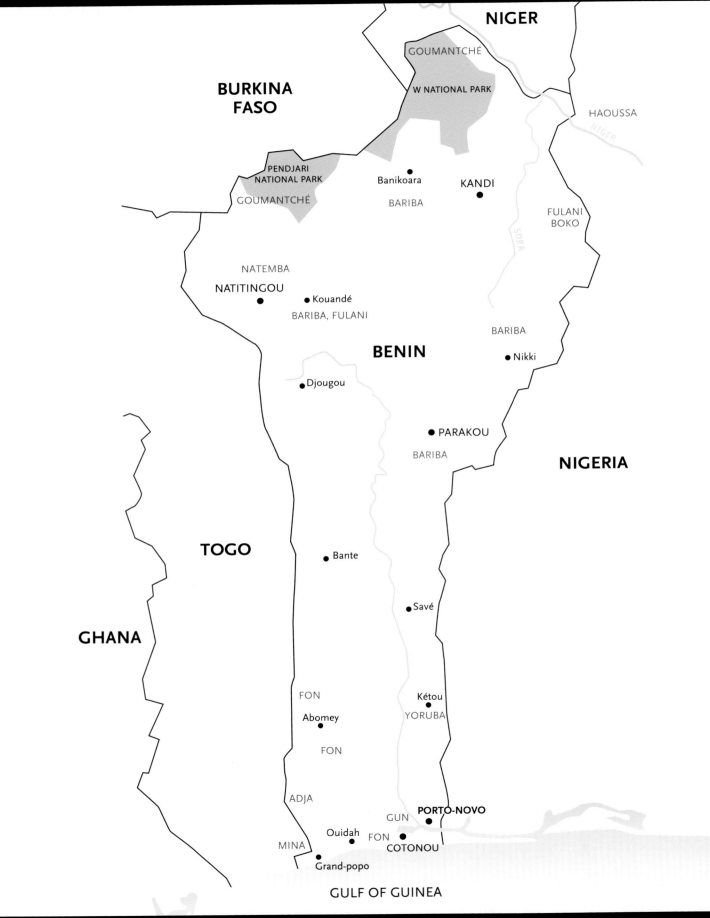

NIGER

BURKINA
FASO

GOUMANTCHÉ

W NATIONAL PARK

HAOUSSA

NIGER

PENDJARI
NATIONAL PARK

Banikoara

KANDI

GOUMANTCHÉ

BARIBA

FULANI
BOKO

SORA

NATEMBA

NATITINGOU

Kouandé

BARIBA, FULANI

BENIN

BARIBA

Nikki

Djougou

PARAKOU

BARIBA

NIGERIA

TOGO

Bante

Savé

GHANA

Kétou

YORUBA

FON

Abomey

FON

ADJA

GUN

PORTO-NOVO

Ouidah

FON

MINA

COTONOU

Grand-popo

GULF OF GUINEA

Benin
A cloth of blue

The small republic of Benin (formerly the kingdom of Dahomey) is shaped a bit like a *pagne* or traditional cloth wrap – it seems to hang down from the arid region of Burkina Faso to the north, between Togo to the west and Nigeria to the east, and its lower fringes dip into the Atlantic Ocean.

There are traces of some forty ethnic groups in Benin, a country which was ruled at one time from Abomey – a period of great turbulence in its history – and a victim of the slave trade that transported West Africans in great numbers to Brazil and Haiti.

I got to know Benin through an organization set up to promote the traditional technique of indigo dyeing. With Nicolas as my guide, I followed the story of cotton, step by step, in the stifling backstreets of Cotonou's old quarter and the dust-reddened expanses of the bush. I met the people who do the spinning and weaving, and the dyeing and cutting and sewing, coming into direct contact with those age-old techniques whose richness has inspired contemporary fashion designers, both in Africa and internationally.

Indigo skies, indigo seas

Cotton and indigo *The perfect pair*

Cotton and indigo make good neighbours: the flower of one produces a beautiful natural-coloured cloth; the leaf of the other dyes it a deep and sublime blue.

Below: Indigo plant.

Nicolas is in charge of production for the firm of Heartwear, in Cotonou.

Cotton grows in the north of Benin. It is picked and de-seeded by hand and woven in small workshops on narrow looms, or alternatively conveyed to a factory in big trucks that scatter a carpet of white tufts over the roadsides. From here, it will emerge in the form of undyed cretonne, in 120 cm panels – the width of a *pagne*, or traditional cloth wrap.

Dehana runs a women's cooperative in Djougou and she explains how the cotton is de-seeded prior to weaving: 'I spread out a ball of cotton on a flat stone, then I use a metal roller to crush it and get rid of the seeds.' The cotton is then carded and spun using a stick weighted with a ball of baked clay and the same hand motions that have been used worldwide and for generation after generation.

The West African indigo plant, *Lonchocarpus cyanescens*, grows wild in the bush. Indigo dyeing is an ancient technique, but it is fast disappearing and indigo cloth is being replaced by wax-printed cloth, which is better suited to contemporary styles of dress. Tourism, however, keeps the tradition alive.

Left: Arafi, a Yoruba dyer, holding two balls of indigo and some of the bark that is used in the dye mixture.

Below left: In cooperatives like the one Dehana runs in Djougou, the cotton is hand spun before being woven into panels on a narrow loom.

Opposite, centre right: A heap of raw cotton, piled beneath a tree. Although most West African countries grow cotton, the markets are flooded with Chinese exports.

Opposite, below right: Lucienne, a dyer from Sokponta, unfolds a *pagne* in cotton damask.

In Cotonou, the dyers work in privately run concessions in the Scoagbéto district. Women tie their cloth ready for dyeing before they bring it along, and all the cloth goes into the dye vat at the same time, each individual piece identified by the owner's 'signature', which is tied into a corner of fabric. When the cloth comes out of the vat, it is dark green and after being rinsed, it is soaked again until it acquires the correct depth of colour. It is hung, still bound and dripping, in the concession's yard, then when it is dry, the ties are removed and the final pattern is revealed.

Indigo dyeing is also used for a type of cloth known as cotton damask, a factory-produced fabric made using mercerized cotton thread on a Jacquard loom. The motifs appear in slight relief, in the same colour as the background.

Lucienne practises hand dyeing in Sokponta. 'The sad thing,' she says, 'is that young people don't even know what indigo looks like when it's growing wild in the bush.' Like many other dyers here, she gives cotton damask – originally from Germany or China – an African flavour by decorating it with tie-dyed patterns in multiple colours.

Arafi, a Yoruba dyer, describes the dyeing process:

'*I crush the indigo leaves in a mortar until they form a paste, then shape the paste into balls and leave them to dry in the sun. Then I dissolve them in water with some ash in it, cover the mixture and put it to one side. I give it an occasional stir and wait for a green film to appear on the surface. If I try the mixture and it tastes bitter, that means the dye is ready. I soak the cloth in it, then rinse it and leave it to dry, and if it's not dark enough, I repeat the process.*'

Studded with stars, spots and stripes

In Benin, indigo cloth may be decorated with masses of little dots – reminiscent of the night sky – or with broad stripes like the patterns of traditional facial scarification. Both of these patterns are created with the tie-dye technique. Haoussa men prefer to dye the thread itself prior to weaving their gorgeous pagnes and striped boubous.

Starry indigo

The stippled or star-studded effects of the indigo galaxy are produced by the tie-dye or *plangi* technique, which involves knotting the fabric in a particular pattern, then dyeing it.

After stopping off at a spinning mill to buy some raw cloth, Nicolas takes me to a village that specializes in tying fabric to make *pagnes*. Here, we meet Alfred, who is responsible for distributing the work to the various 'tiers', each of whom has a pattern she particularly likes working on.

I watch Mathilde drawing a few guide marks on her material using a piece of charcoal, then taking some plastic wire salvaged from a bag of rice and pinching a bit of fabric between her thumb and index finger and tying it to form a series of single, double or triple cones, spacing the cones according to the pattern. By inserting a pebble, a cowrie shell or a seed into the pinched section of fabric before tying, she can also vary the size and shape of the design.

It takes up to a week to tie the cloth; then the scrunched fabric is taken to the dye vats in Cotonou. Six yards, or approximately 5.5 metres, of fabric will make a *pagne*; 12 yards, or 11.5 metres, will make a *complet* or three-piece outfit, which includes a matching top, skirt and headscarf.

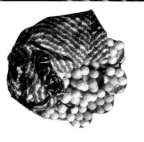

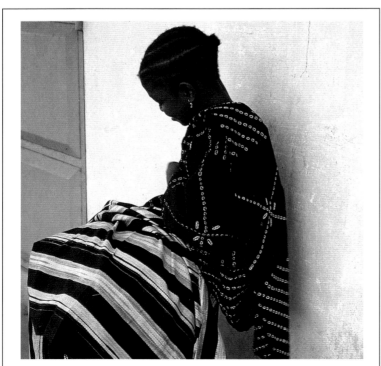

Plangi and *tritik*. Julienne's dress is decorated with a *plangi* pattern, but the stripes on the cloth have been sewn and dyed using a technique known as *tritik*. After the fabric has been dyed (and dried), it is Julienne's job to unpick the stitches – a slow process.

Above: Fabric tied by Mathilde.

Opposite, right: Arafi, the dyer, rinses the cloth, then pulls it to break the stitches and reveal the resist pattern underneath.

Right: Cecile is Togolese and lives in Paris. She is wearing a tunic with a peanut-like pattern and carrying a pile of indigo fabrics on her head, variously patterned with checks, stripes, stars, banana leaves and coffee beans.

Far right: A man from the Tatasoumba people with scarified patterns on his face.

Far left: Tied cloth, or *plangi*, prior to dyeing.

Left: Patterns revealed after dyeing and removal of the ties.

Stitching and symmetry

Cotton cloth can also be striped to form various motifs – parallel or intersecting lines, zigzags and chevrons – which resemble the patterns of facial scarification that are used as a ritual means of identification among different ethnic groups. The effect also recalls the designs seen on banco walls, scratched by hand before the mud has had time to dry.

In Zoungo, the tailors' quarter in Cotonou, men are busy sewing amidst the sound of clicking pedals. They are using a decorative technique called *tritik*, which involves machine sewing a length of cloth, using running stitch, whipstitch and zigzag stitch, dyeing it and then removing the stitches to reveal the pattern in negative on the indigo ground. The cloth is folded in half lengthwise and the two layers are stitched together, both to save time and to produce – after dyeing and unpicking – a symmetrical design on either side of the central fold. The stitches are removed by tugging the cloth sharply at both ends to break the thread, and the pattern is magically revealed, a little like a photograph being developed. Then all that remains to be done is to collect up all the broken threads.

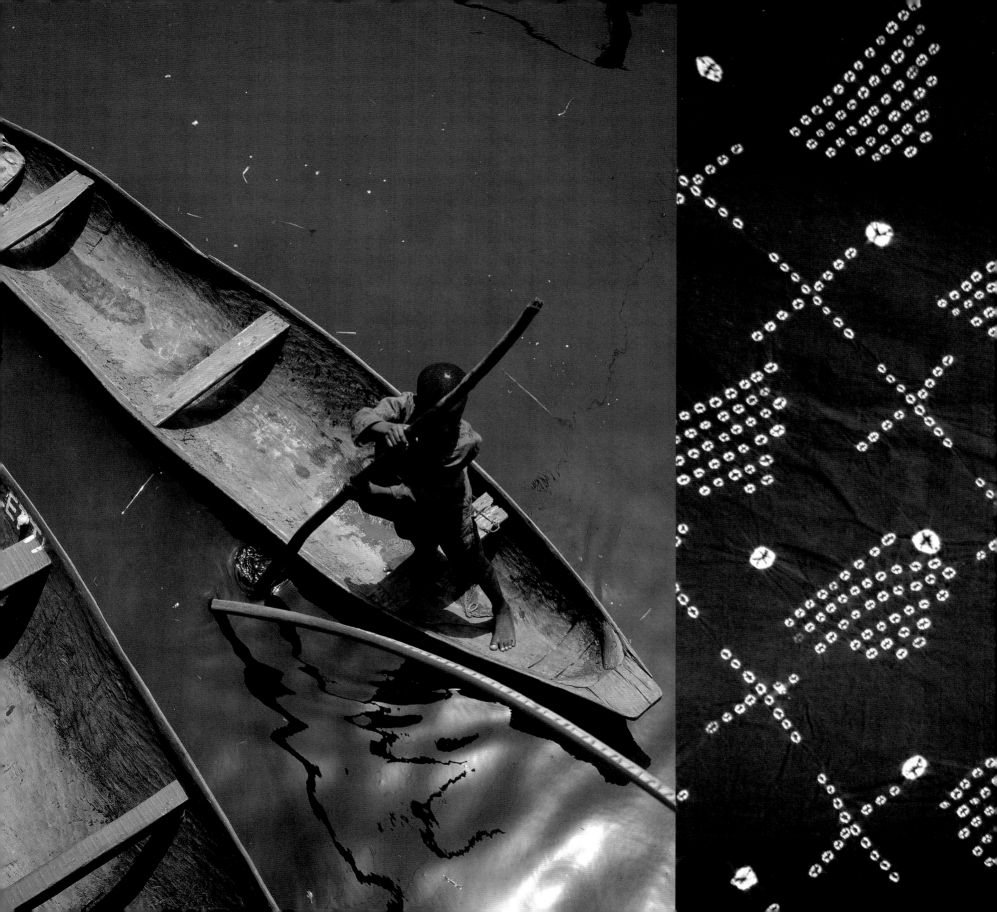

Above: Haoussa *boubou* in striped cotton with white embroidery around the neck and on the chest and back.

Below: Man from the Haoussa tribe selling striped indigo cloth in the market in Parakou, north-east Benin.

Opposite: Examples of Haoussa warp ikat: solid stripes alternate with ikat stripes.

Woven indigo

The Haoussa are Muslims from northern Nigeria and northern Niger. Skilled weavers and dyers, they are also great travellers and traders and sell their indigo cloth on the markets in Benin. The cloth, which is assembled from a number of narrow striped bands, is used to make *pagnes* and also the *boubou* or *agdaba*, a magnificent flowing robe worn by men. Ikat stripes are integrated into the weave, making this a very beautiful garment, the neckline of which is traditionally embroidered with Islamic-inspired arabesques and interlacing designs.

The ikat or *adire* technique consists in tying sections of the thread prior to dyeing. The tied thread is dyed in a ditch outside the village rather than in a basin or vat. Like weaving and embroidery, the job of dyeing is primarily done by men.

The ties are then removed and the dyed thread is strung on the loom. The tying of the warp threads creates resist-dyed areas that are clearly delimited widthwise but fuzzy and ill-defined lengthwise; these are repeated at regular intervals according to the chosen pattern of tying.

The stripes of varying widths, in shades of indigo ranging from light blue to black, the vibrancy of the ikat threads and the intricate white embroidery that is added later all combine to make the Haoussa *boubou* a spectacular garment with a very contemporary feel.

Tied ikat yarn or adire.

1. Tied yarn prior to dyeing.   2. Dyed yarn.   3. Yarn after removal of the ties.

Colours of West Africa

Wax prints and fancy prints

Clothes can tell you a great deal about a person and pagnes *are no exception to this rule. Some printed patterns have special names and symbolic meanings, which speak volumes about the African woman's world.*

The quality of the fabric, the maker's mark printed on the selvedge, the price, colour and symbolism of the design may all be part of a coded message. There is one popular *pagne* design known as 'the eye of my rival', and another known as 'my husband's pack animal'; there are *pagnes* decorated with mobile phones, fans, peanuts and fish. There are also commemorative *pagnes* decorated with portraits of local politicians or Queen Elizabeth II, or designs that celebrate major festivals or sporting events.

Above: Two local handicrafts: pottery and wax prints.

Right: A Beninese potter from the village of Sé, wearing a blouse, headscarf and *pagne* in three different wax print patterns.

Opposite: Men and women attending the Vaudoun festival in Grand Popo, wearing their finest wax print *pagnes* and *boubous*.

To follow the history of the wax-print *pagne*, we have to travel right round the globe, starting in the 19th century with the arrival of Dutch settlers on the Indonesian island of Java. The batik designs used by Javanese craftsmen for their sarongs appealed to the Dutch, who soon began mass-producing cloth resembling authentic batik and selling it to the local population. The Indonesian craftsmen themselves followed suit, learning how to adapt their skills and produce their cloth mechanically.

Ghanaian soldiers enlisted by the Dutch East India Company returned home bearing Javanese sarongs, and these became so popular that the Dutch redirected their trade towards the Gold Coast, as Ghana was then known. It was from these interchanges that a major element of West Africa's cultural identity was born: the wax print.

This man is dressed for the Awalé festival in a smart, if rather unusual, combination of bowler hat, woven *boubou* and a wax print shawl.

The wax print is a mass-produced cloth, of Dutch origin, whose technique and design are inspired by the Indonesian batik method of wax-resist. The cloth passes between two rollers, which print the wax on both sides, and is then immersed in a dye bath. On authentic wax prints, it is usual to find little bubbles and streaks of colour, caused tiny cracks in the wax.

When the wax has been melted off, other colours are applied by hand, using printing pads.

The cloth known as fancy print, or imiwax, is a wax print imitation that creates a similar effect without the use of wax. Quality wax prints are produced by Vlisco, in Helmond, the Netherlands, and also in Manchester, England. Since becoming independent, African countries (which already produce their own cotton) have opened their own spinning mills and printing factories, such as Comatex in Mali and Enitex in Niger. Today's markets, however, are being destabilized by the importation of cheap wax prints and fancy prints from China, India and Pakistan.

The appeal of wax prints and fancy prints lies in their bright colours, multiple motifs and marbled effects, and they are a common sight in the streets of Cotonou, and all over West Africa. The women of Benin, Togo and Mali are by no means ready to swap their *pagne* for a pair of jeans, and a whole generation of African designers, led by Chris Seydou from Mali, have succeeded in renewing interest in local textile and craft traditions, bringing African fashion into the spotlight.

Opposite and overleaf: A selection of the vibrant coloured prints worn by both men and women across West Africa.

Glossary

alizarin: red dye extracted from madder root; now chemically produced.

appliqué: technique that involves sewing a piece of fabric onto a base fabric for decorative purposes.

backstrap loom: mobile loom where the warp yarns are attached to a belt that goes round the weaver's back. Also called a belt loom.

bandhani: Indian name for tie-dye.

batik: dye-resist technique that uses hot wax to create patterned areas impervious to the dye.

bias: a diagonal across the grain of a fabric. Because of its stretchiness, bias-cut fabric can be used to make a curved section of a garment such as a neckline.

brandenburg: roll of decorative braid used as a fastening or trimming.

brocade: woven fabric with a supplementary weft pattern.

broderie anglaise: openwork embroidery in the same shade as the base fabric.

calendering: technique for giving a sheen to a fabric. Indigo-dyed cloth is coated with egg white or blood, then beaten with a wooden mallet until it becomes shiny.

chain stitch: embroidery stitch resembling the links of a chain.

charpoy: Indian bed made of woven webbing stretched on a wooden frame.

cotton damask: factory-produced damasked cloth woven on a Jacquard loom using mercerized yarn.

cowrie: type of shell, commonly used for decorative purposes.

cretonne: heavy, ribbed cotton fabric

distaff: rod on which cotton or wool is wound before spinning.

fancy print: African term for cotton cloth printed with rollers to resemble a wax print.

futon: cotton mattress traditionally used in Japan.

ginning: removal of seeds and impurities from cotton prior to weaving.

ikat: technique that involves resist-dyeing thread prior to weaving. It may involve the warp threads (warp ikat), the weft threads (weft ikat) or both (double or compound ikat).

jaspe/jaspeado: name for the ikat technique in Central America.

khadi: Indian cotton, spun and woven by hand.

lehariya: Indian style of tie-dye, in which the fabric is tied on the diagonal.

lurex: thin metallic thread coated with plastic to give it a shiny look.

magnanery: building where silkworms are bred.

mercerized: (of cotton yarn) treated with a caustic alkali solution to give it a lustrous silky appearance.

mordant: substance used to fix dye. Lime, ash and urine are all natural mordants.

organdie: fine cotton muslin.

organza: thrown silk used to form a warp.

pagne: name used in French-speaking West Africa for a multipurpose cloth that may be worn as a skirt, scarf or headdress.

percale: close-textured woven cotton fabric, sometimes with a glazed finish like chintz.

piastre: former monetary unit of Indochina during colonial times, now used as an ornamental decoration.

poplin: plain-weave cotton fabric with fine ribbing.

printing: process in which a motif is transferred to a textile. Methods include block printing, copperplate printing, roller printing and silkscreen printing.

ramie: *Boehmeria nivea*, a plant whose fibres are woven to produce a fabric that is lighter than hemp.

rayon: shiny synthetic fabric made from a form of cellulose.

retting: process of separating hemp fibres by destroying the sticky substance (pectin) that holds them together.

reverse appliqué: technique that consists in superimposing two or more layers of fabric in contrasting colours, then cutting the top fabric to reveal the colours of the lower layers. The edges of the cut fabric are turned under and hemmed to create a pattern.

salwar kameez: outfit composed of tunic and trousers, often matching, worn by both men and women in South Asia.

sapek: former monetary unit used in China; it has a hole in the centre and is now used decoratively.

selvedge: the edge of a woven fabric where the weft turns and runs back: this edge does not unravel.

sequin: small perforated metal disc sewn on to a garment for decoration.

skein: length of yarn wound in a coil and tied.

soutache: narrow woven or crocheted braid used as a decorative trimming.

supplementary weft: an extra weft thread woven in to create a motif or repeat pattern.

tie-dye: resist-dyeing technique that involves knotting a section of fabric with string or thread prior to dyeing, so that a negative pattern is produced. Tie-dye techniques used around the world include *plangi* (Indonesia), *bandhani* (India) and *shibori* (Japan).

torque: type of rigid necklace.

tritik: dye-resist technique, which involves folding and sewing the fabric before dyeing.

turmeric: plant whose roots can be used to create a yellow dye.

warp: the set of yarns that are stretched lengthwise on a loom.

wax print: cotton fabric that has been printed with wax on both sides, then dyed to create a resist pattern.

weft: the yarn that runs across a loom, through the warp threads.

Bibliography

Indigo
Jenny Balfour-Paul
London: British Museum Press, 1998

The Way of the World
Nicolas Bouvier
Edinburgh: Polygon, 1992

Beadwork: A World Guide
Caroline Crabtree and Pam Stallebrass
London: Thames & Hudson, 2002

Ethnic Style: History and Fashion
Bérénice Geoffroy-Schneiter
New York: Assouline, 2001

World Textiles
John Gillow and Bryan Sentance
London: Thames & Hudson, 1999

The Art of the Loom
Ann Hecht
London: British Museum Press, 1989

Ethnic Dress
Frances Kennett
New York: Facts on File, 1995

The Shining Cloth
Victoria Z. Rivers
London: Thames & Hudson, 1999

Costume Patterns and Designs
Max Tilke
New York: Rizzoli, 1990

 ## Africa

Tissus d'Afrique
Claude Fauque and Otto Wollenweber
Paris:
Syros-Alternatives, 1994

Printed and Dyed Textiles from Africa
John Gillow
London:
British Museum Press, 2001

African Textiles: Colour and Creativity Across a Continent
John Gillow
London:
Thames & Hudson, 2003

L'Afrique des textiles
Anne Grosfilley
Aix-en-Provence: Édisud, 2004

 ## Asia

All extracts from poems are taken from:

Chants-Poèmes des monts et des eaux: Anthologie des littératures orales des ethnies du Vietnam
Mireille Gansel, foreword by Georges Condominas
Paris: Sudestasie/Unesco, 1986

Costumes traditionnels de la Chine du Sud-Est
Éric Boudot, Lionel Henry, Marie-Paule Raibaud, Marie-Hélène Guelton and Marie-Claire Quiquemelle (exhibition catalogue)
Lyons: Musée des Tissus, 2002

North East Vietnam: Mountains and Ethnic Minorities
Tim Doling
Hanoi: Thê Gioi Publishers, 2000

Miao Textiles from China
Gina Corrigan
London: British Museum Press, 2001

The Vanishing Tribes of Burma
Richard K. Diran
London: Seven Dials, 1999

De fil et d'argent. Mémoire des Miao de Chine
Philippe Fatin Collection
Nice: Musée des Arts Asiatiques, 2004

Chine du Sud: La Mosaïque des minorités
Françoise Grenot-Wang
Paris: Les Indes Savantes, 2001

Montagnards des Pays d'Indochine
Christine Hemmet
Boulogne-Billancourt: Éditions Sépia, 1995

Le Viêt Nam des Royaumes: Modes et esthétique chez les minorités du Viêt Nam
Christine Hemmet
Paris:
Éditions Cercle d'Art, 1995

Vietnam, 1975–2005
'Population' by Christine Hemmet
GEO Magazine, special issue, 2005

Peoples of the Golden Triangle
Paul and Elaine Lewis
London:
Thames & Hudson, 1984

A Yao Community in Sapa, Vietnam
Vo Mai Phuong and Claire Burkert
Hanoi:
Vietnam Museum of Ethnology, 2001

The Yao: The Mien and Mun Yao in China, Vietnam, Laos and Thailand
Jess G. Pourret
London: Thames & Hudson, 2002

Brodeurs de Brume: Les Miao de la Chine secrète
Annie Reffet
Paris: Éditions Soline, 1999

Vietnam, au pays des routes contraires
Gérard Rovillé and Xavier Zimbardo
Paris: Éditions Peuples du Monde, 1994

Catalogue of the Vietnam Museum of Ethnology
Hanoi, 1997

Vietnam: Image of the Community of 54 Ethnic Groups
Hanoi: VNA Publishing House, 2000

The Museum of the Cultures of Vietnam's Ethnic Groups
Hanoi: Cultures of Nationalities Publishing, 1997

 ## Guatemala and Mexico

Threads of Identity
Patricia B. Altman and Caroline D. West
Los Angeles: UCLA Fowler Museum of Cultural History, 1992

Textiles du Guatemala
Régis Bertrand
Paris: Arthaud, 1992

Indian Costumes from Guatemala
Krystyna Deuss
London:
K. Deuss, 1981

Textiles Mayas
Danielle Dupiech-Cavaleri
Paris:
Éditions Unesco, 1999

Maya-Textilien aus Guatemala
Gitta Hassler
Stuttgart:
Arnoldsch, 2006

The Maya of Guatemala: Life and Dress
Carmen L. Pettersen
Seattle: University of Washington Press, 1977

Textiles of Central and South America
Angela Thompson
Marlborough: Crowood Press, 2006

 ## India

Tribes of India
Tiziana and Gianni Baldizzone
New Delhi: Bookwise, 2000

Ikat Textiles of India
Chelna Desai
San Francisco: Chronicle Books, 1988

India Sutra: On the Magic Trail of Textiles
Bérénice Ellena
Gurgaon: Shubhi Publications, 2007

Mud, Mirror and Thread
Nora Fisher (ed.)
Middletown, NJ: Grantha Corporation, 1993

Threads of Identity: Embroidery and Adornment of the Nomadic Rabaris
Judy Frater
Ahmedabad: Mapin, 1995

Rajasthan
Pauline van Lynden
New Delhi: Timeless Books, 2003

 ## Panama

Tableaux kuna
Michel Perrin
Paris: Arthaud, 1998

The Art of Being Kuna
Mari Lyn Salvador
Los Angeles: UCLA Fowler Museum of Cultural History, 1997

 ## Romania

La Roumanie au petit bonheur
Bernard Houliat
Montsalvy: Éditions Quelque part sur terre, 2000

Maramures, terra incognita
Gil Jouanard
Martel: Éditions du Laquet, 2002

Maramures
Kosei Miya
Bucharest: Humanitas, 2000

Picture credits and acknowledgments

Picture credits

All photographs are by Catherine Legrand.
Illustrations by Satomi Ichikawa
and Anaïs Guéry.

The illustrations for the section on South-East
Asia are by Satomi Ichikawa, with the exception
of the Akha costume. The portrait of the
Benin dyeworker (page 219) is also by
Satomi Ichikawa. All other illustrations
are by Anaïs Guéry.

Acknowledgments

This book is dedicated to Sonia Jimenez,
who was passionate about textiles, and who
disappeared in Guatemala in December 2003.
I also dedicate it to Yves, my companion in life
and on my travels, and to Sarah, Lola and Mado,
who supported this project.

Many thanks to my friends Pierre Lejeune
in Guatemala, Prakash Detha in Rajasthan,
Yves Venot and Daniel Cendron in Benin,
and Satomi Ichikawa, who was ready for
any challenge.

My best wishes to the guides, drivers and
boatmen who accompanied me: Juan in
Guatemala, Nicolas in Benin, Ngoc and
Dong in Vietnam.

My thanks to all the craftspeople, textile
cooperatives and associations who welcomed
me: El Camino and San Jolobil in San Cristobal
de las Casas, Mexico; Santa Ana in Zunil,
Guatemala; Heartwear in Benin; Brigitte Singh
in Jaipur, Rajasthan, and to everyone else who
helped me with contacts.

For their advice, support and proofreading,
I would like to thank Françoise Cousin, curator
of textiles at the Musée du Quai Branly, Paris,
and Christine Hemmet, director of the Asian
collections at the Musée du Quai Branly.

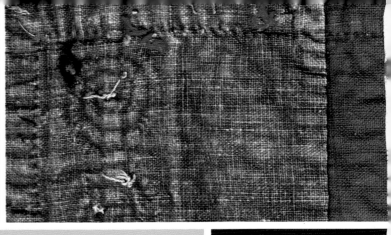

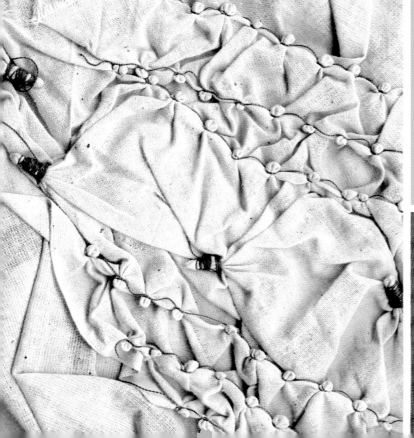
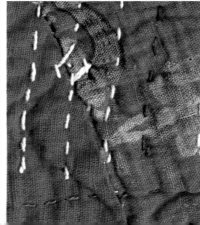
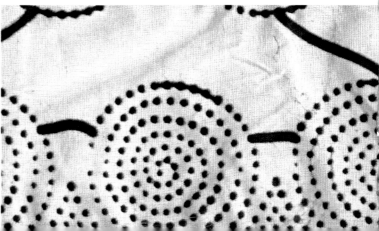

Translated from the French *Textiles et vêtements du monde* by Ruth Sharman

First published in the United Kingdom in 2008 by
Thames & Hudson Ltd, 181A High Holborn, London WC1V 7QX

www.thamesandhudson.com

Original edition © 2008 Aubanel, an imprint of Éditions Minerva, Geneva
This edition @ 2008 Thames & Hudson Ltd, London

British Library Cataloguing-in-Publication Data
A catalogue record for this book is available from the British Library

ISBN 978-0-500-51439-9

Printed and bound in China